MW00789671

AT ALL COSTS

THE TRUE STORY OF VIETNAM WAR HERO DICK ETCHBERGER

Hilary – Enjoy this story of my hero! Cory Etch

MATT PROIETTI

Rick Etch

Copyright © 2015, CMSGT Richard Etchberger
Foundation & Matthew P. Proietti

ISBN: 978-0-9860831-0-5

Library of Congress Control Number: 2014919165

All rights reserved. No part of this book may be reproduced or
transmitted in any form or by any means, electronic or mechanical,
including photocopying, recording, or by any information storage
and retrieval system without written permission from the author,
except for the inclusion of brief quotations in a review.

Printed in the United States of America.

To America's Vietnam War veterans

"A man of character in peace is a man of courage in war."

Lord Moran
AKA Dr. Charles McMoran Wilson
Physician to Winston Churchill
and World War I Royal Army
Medical Corps veteran

Author's Acknowledgment

This book started as an assignment handed down to me in a temporary job I had in 2008 running the Air Force news team in Washington, D.C. I was new to this position, but not to the work. I've
been in the service since 1984 and a reservist since 1988. I've always
been in the same career field, Public Affairs, working primarily as a print
journalist, which I also did as a civilian for nine years.

I was unfamiliar with the name of Chief Master Sgt. Richard
L. Etchberger, Project Heavy Green or the Air Force's larger Combat
Skyspot ground-directed bombing mission during the Vietnam War
when my boss, Lt. Col. Melinda Fay Morgan, told me Etchberger
might be nominated for the Medal of Honor. We needed to look into
his background to have a story about him ready to go if the decoration
was approved.

After trying to assign it to three younger writers on the staff only to
have each suggest that I do it instead because of my appreciation for Air
Force history, I took off a Friday and drove up to the chief's hometown
of Hamburg, Pennsylvania, with my wife, Varina. I had arranged to
interview two of his childhood classmates, June Kline and Don Yocom,
at a cafe. June has a scrapbook of things related to her late friend's life,
and we flipped through that together while they told me what he was
like as a teenager, not as a war hero or even much as an adult.

A bit of magic happened as we sat there. One of them mentioned
that Dick had an older brother, Robert. Then Don looked up from the
table and said, "There he is." A man in his 70s with a full head of snow-
white hair was heading straight toward us from the door. He walked

up, pointed to me and said, "I was told to come here to talk to you." I figured this was just small town life: he'd heard that an Air Force writer was in town to learn about his brother and came by to offer some insight. While that's true, Robert Etchberger hadn't lived in Hamburg for some time. He was simply visiting from his home in Florida for a few days for a high school reunion. What luck!

We later visited Dick Etchberger's grave and found a laminated letter to him left by someone who had served under him more than 40 years earlier. June and Don brought me to a memorial Hamburg had dedicated to Etch a few years before. It was clear to me that what made him special as a career GI had its start in his hometown.

After just one day on the trail of this story, I knew one piece wouldn't be enough. It would take a series to do it justice. My time in Washington soon came to a close, and I wrote three stories on Etch that fall on my own time at home in California. One day I got an email from his youngest son, Cory, then living in Bern, Switzerland, with his wife and daughter. He'd heard I was looking into his father's career and offered to help. I was delighted, of course, and we exchanged emails through that fall and winter. In early 2009, he mentioned he had been thinking about writing a book about his father and casually asked if I would be interested in helping him. I said that I would and believed there was enough there for a book, whether or not his father ever received the Medal of Honor.

We met in Switzerland that spring, which I mention for no other reason than it sounds glamorous for me to have gone to Europe for a book project. Truthfully, I was doing some Air Force work in Germany then, and it was an easy train ride away. I spent a day reviewing Dick Etchberger's military records, deciphering them for Cory. That was the beginning. We tried writing together but both quickly realized this was a one-person job—and I was him. It took a lot of trust for Cory to turn over the project to me, and I admire him for that. I believe it was the right decision to have his father's story told by someone not so close to it.

I had one goal when I started this book: to tell Dick Etchberger's story accurately and not make him out to be superhuman. We glorify athletes, musicians, actors, etc., to the point where their achievements seem beyond our reach. They aren't, not even for war heroes. There are people serving today who undertake actions worthy of the Medal of Honor if such a situation presents itself. It rarely does. That's why it sits atop each service's chart of decorations.

So, first, I'd like to thank Cory for inviting me to participate in his project, which soon became my own. I'd also like to thank him for his encouragement; his patience as I explored various avenues, few of which thankfully were dead ends; and for his friendship. Cory is a sweet man, and I know his Dad would be proud of who he has become. I believe that of his brothers, too.

Steve and Rich were also essential to this book, though they let Cory take the lead in being the family's contact with me. Being the eldest, Steve knew their Dad the best and shared details about Etch's personality that helped me paint a clearer picture of who he was as a father and husband. This was just as important for me to understand as what he had achieved as a GI. Brother three, Rich Etchberger is sharp, sharp, sharp. I didn't bug him nearly as much as I did Cory or even Steve, but he was always quick to reply with his ideas when I reached out to him. It was clear to me throughout that he thought his father's story deserved a wider audience and that he expected me to take that responsibility seriously. I think I have and, more importantly, I believe Rich thinks so, too.

My wife, Varina, has been at my side since day one of this project: she accompanied me to Hamburg during that first visit in 2008. She has been supportive, encouraging and usually was the first person to read my chapters, which I wrote largely out of order. When she didn't understand something in the story, she asked. She's very bright and incredibly well-read so when she doesn't grasp something in a story, that's a problem for the writer. At times Vee served as my unpaid research assistant, particularly at the Lyndon B. Johnson Presidential Library in Austin, Texas, which we visited multiple times. This book wouldn't be what it is without her involvement.

Regarding the LBJ Library, I'd be remiss not to thank archivist John Wilson and the rest of the staff there for their kindness. They treated me as a serious writer from the beginning, even though I arrived wearing a t-shirt, shorts and flip-flops to just see about the possibility of doing some research there in the future. Over my protests at my attire, one of the clerks insisted I speak right then to Mr. Wilson, who happened to be free. He asked about my project and when I mentioned Etchberger's name, his eyes lit up and he said, "Lima Site 85." I was stunned that he knew the name of the secret location in Laos where Etch and his teammates had worked. Mr. Wilson didn't just point me in the right direction to materials that would help me: he knew off the top of his head what specific boxes I needed to review to round out my story so readers grasped how Project Heavy Green was planned with the knowledge of the highest levels of Washington, D.C.

Seeing this project through to the end gives me a deeper appreciation for those writers who tackle nonfiction work. This wasn't just writing a book where all of the facts were fairly easy to come by, which would have been difficult in itself. This was akin to putting together a jigsaw puzzle when you're not sure how many pieces there are and, in fact, the number keeps growing as details are added to the borders.

I'd also like to thank Peter Collier, author of *Medal of Honor: Portraits of Valor Beyond the Call of Duty*. We live near each other in Northern California, and he was kind enough to meet me for coffee early on in my writing. I had an idea of where I was headed and, after hearing it from me, Mr. Collier confirmed that he thought my gut feeling was the way to proceed. His confidence meant a lot to me.

My Air Force Reserve friend Ray Sarracino, a former *USA Today* graphics' professional, designed the front and back covers, plus the Southeast Asia map readers will consult. Ray is a fine senior noncommissioned officer who also worked part time on the Washington, D.C., news team where the idea for this book started. His delight at participating in *At All Costs* was touching.

Lastly, I'd like to thank my parents, siblings, former public school teachers and the library staff in my hometown of Leominster, Massachusetts, for instilling in me a love for the written word, and the Air Force for giving me a platform through which to develop it. Frankly, I'm grateful to anyone who has given me even the slightest encouragement about my writing through the years.

—Matt Proietti, March 2015

Foreword

by Rich Etchberger

Two telephone calls bookend most of my memories of my father. The first one was on March 12, 1968, and it was devastating. The second was on July 7, 2010, and it was liberating. During the 42 years that separated those calls, much of what I had learned about the last months and days of Dad's life turned out to not be true. However, the one fact that could not be altered was that he was gone from my life.

I was raised in a close-knit United States Air Force family during the early years of the war in Southeast Asia. I, my older brother Steve and my younger brother Cory thoroughly enjoyed the adventure of frequent family moves between air bases around the world. In 1965, we took up residence at Clark Air Force Base in the Philippines. During this time, Dad was often gone for long periods of time, but my mother, Catherine, kept the show running smoothly at home. Mom was a supportive Air Force wife and a strong backer of Dad's career. Cory and I spent our free time playing army, chasing lizards and riding our bikes. I started my Little League baseball career there, playing second base for the Clark Colts. When Dad would return from his trips, he would take Cory and me to the base barber shop where we would request three military-style buzz cuts. To share his Air Force life with us, Dad would often bring home some bits of military gear like a web belt, a canteen or an air mattress for us to play with. Our brother Steve soon started his career in the Air Force and was stationed in Southern California, where he worked as an aircraft mechanic. Life seemed pretty normal to me.

The adventure was tempered in 1967 when we moved to Chanute Air Force Base in Illinois, where Cory and I attended public school.

It was a major change for us as we had never attended a school that was not on a military base. It was there that I experienced my first bloody nose during a playground fistfight and heard the first racist taunts of my young life. We had always lived among a diversity of people and had embraced their cultures. Living in Illinois tested my 4th-grade vision of what the world should be. Much later in life, I learned that my Dad was not pleased with that assignment either. It seemed like a miracle when we suddenly left Illinois for Dad's hometown of Hamburg, Pennsylvania. We quickly adapted to life off of an Air Force base, mostly because of the love and attention of our grandparents. The Etchberger family was well known in Hamburg as my grandfather managed a small general store downtown. Dad had been a popular student and had many friends in the community. As he disappeared, once again, on a military assignment in fall 1967 our house at 769 State St. in Hamburg became our base as Cory and I made new friends and explored our surroundings.

When I answered the telephone on that fateful night in March 1968, our lives as a military family ended. For most of my life, I believed what the Air Force officer had told my mother on the phone. The following years were marked by doubt and confusion for me. I had always loved the Air Force way of life and at an early age had planned to someday follow in my father's footsteps. However, the late 1960s and early 1970s were turbulent times in the United States and I was abruptly exposed to the dissent surrounding the war. As my high school graduation approached, I knew that my future would not include being a part of the Air Force. During the ensuing years, I have often wondered how my life could have been different if it were not for that phone call.

As time went by, Mom told me many stories about her early life with Dad, including how they had met at a small cafe in Salt Lake City, Utah. She recounted many happy times with Dad living in Morocco, North Dakota and the Philippines. But she never spoke about their life after we left Illinois in 1967. At the time, it did not seem strange, as I know she suffered the pain greatly. She would not share any details of Dad's secret life with me until the week of my wedding in August 1994. Sadly, Mom died a month later, taking many facts about her life with Dad to the grave with her. When Cory answered the phone call from President Obama on July 7, 2010, it would open the door for those secrets to be revealed, not just to us but to a nation.

1

Robert Etchberger was astounded as he looked in the casket holding the body of his younger brother. The military had told the family that Dick, a career Air Force sergeant, had died in a helicopter crash related to the Vietnam War just days after his 35th birthday. Yet here were his remains looking remarkably as if he were simply asleep. His handsome face showed no scratches or bruising. He was freshly shaven and wearing a new dress blue uniform.

Four years older than Dick, Bob returned to live in the brothers' hometown of Hamburg, Pennsylvania, after serving four years in the Navy. He had arranged for the mortuary staff to call him when the body arrived so he could view it ahead of his parents and sister-in-law.

"I didn't want my mother subjected to something I didn't want her to see," he said.

Kay Etchberger had been told about her husband's death by phone. She sank to the floor in agony, her world shattered just hours after she had received a joyous call from her oldest son, Steven, in California telling her that she had become a first-time grandmother. The *Hamburg Item* newspaper reported that Dick, based in Thailand, had been killed in a helicopter crash. That initial account was purposefully inaccurate, a planted story by the Defense Department to cover up what had really happened. Although Dick was based in Thailand for part of his time in Southeast Asia, the rest of it had been spent working at a clandestine U.S. radar site in Laos, a country that was officially neutral in the war. The circumstances of his March 1968 death on a mountaintop where the CIA had a simple landing strip—and the loss of 11 of his comrades, most of whom's bodies were never recovered—would not be acknowledged publicly by the military for many years. It was the Air Force's greatest loss of ground personnel in the war, and few people knew of it for four decades. Except for his wife, his survivors had little information about his death. Kay knew much more than she let on, keeping the full story from her sons for many years.

Etchberger's body was accompanied home from overseas by his commander, Col. Jerry Clayton, who had been in the Air Force since even before it became a separate service from the Army in 1947. Vietnam was the third war for Clayton, who flew bombers in World War II and Korea before becoming a radar officer in the 1950s. He was new to the "spook" business of secret operations, though, and he was shaken by the loss of his men on a mountain peak 12 miles outside of North Vietnam. Clayton shadowed Etch's remains home on a military refueling aircraft, all but sneaking them back into the country due to the secret nature of the men's mission. The body was among 50 or so on the tanker, a so-called "flying gas station" pushed into somber service as an airborne hearse because American GIs were dying at such a rate that they were sent home on any plane with available space. Men in a secret office in the Pentagon instructed Clayton to bring Etchberger's body to Hamburg and leave without speaking to his survivors. They also told him what to do when customs officials boarded his airplane at Elmendorf Air Force Base in Anchorage, Alaska.

"(They said) when they come up the steps, the first guy is our guy. He'll look at you and you look at him. You just nod your head and that's all," said Clayton. "He came up there and they looked around, said nothing and got off the airplane. I literally smuggled Dick into the country."

Etchberger's body was delivered to Delaware's Dover Air Force Base, home to the Defense Department's mortuary affairs center. The staff prepared it for viewing by his loved ones. They trimmed his hair to within regulation length, clothed him in a new uniform and knotted a tie around his neck. They attached chrome U.S. insignia to each collar and, above the left breast pocket, neatly lined a rack of decorations he had earned in his 16-year career. On each sleeve they sewed the stripes of a chief master sergeant, the highest enlisted rank in the Air Force. They stretched new socks over his feet and put on fresh black shoes.

The military arranged for a Hamburg funeral parlor to send a hearse and driver 120 miles to Dover to retrieve the body and return it to Berks County northwest of Philadelphia. Etchberger had moved his wife and two youngest sons to his hometown the previous summer when he joined the mission that would cost him his life. Steven, Kay's son from her first marriage, had followed in his stepfather's path and was serving in the Air Force in California. It was his young bride who had given birth about the time her father-in-law was killed. Clayton and the driver said little to each other as the latter guided the vehicle north past the farms of Delaware and into eastern Pennsylvania until, after a journey around a third of the world, Etchberger's body arrived at the Burkey & Spacht Funeral Home just steps away from the general store run by his father and the bank where his brother worked. As the staff tended to the casket, Clayton wandered down Fourth Street and peered into Miller's 5 & 10. He imagined the late sergeant as a teen 20 years earlier, stocking shelves and scooping ice cream just as his older brother had done before him. Clayton soon climbed back into the passenger seat of the hearse and caught a ride to Washington, D.C., to see his family and report to the Pentagon about what had gone so wrong with Project Heavy Green.

2

On Sept. 7, 1967, the U.S. Air Force invited 40 of its top radar technicians and electronics officers to a secret meeting at Barksdale Air Force Base near Shreveport, Louisiana. Their orders simply said they were to attend a "special briefing." That was an understatement. These select men were being invited to join an undercover assignment that was clandestine even by the standards already in place in Southeast Asia during the Vietnam War. Among the enlisted men was Chief Master Sgt. Dick Etchberger, a 16-year veteran known as a crack radar man and disciplined senior noncommissioned officer. The Pennsylvania native had recently returned from a two-year tour of duty in the Philippines and was settling into a new job outside of his longtime career field when he was sent to the meeting from Chanute Air Force Base, Illinois. With the men gathered in the headquarters of the 1st Combat Evaluation Group (CEVG), Lt. Col. Bob Cornetti from the Air Force's special operations planning office at the Pentagon said everyone in attendance was being considered for a yearlong top secret mission and they had to decide whether to participate before they even knew what it involved.

"Everyone was told (it) was a dangerous and highly classified mission, and once you're told what this is all about, there's no backing out," said Jerry Clayton, the man who was to lead the team. "If you want to back out, you have to do it now."

Only one man did. After he left the room, the others were told that they would run a radar site to help increase the bomb damage the U.S. was inflicting on North Vietnam, particularly around its capital of Hanoi. Clayton had handpicked the men, all of whom were connected to the 1st CEVG, which controlled subordinate units around the world that were part of America's defensive network built up during the Cold War. U.S. President Lyndon B. Johnson had ordered the Pentagon's Joint Chiefs of Staff to improve the bombing results to force North Vietnamese leaders to negotiate an end to the war. Until this time, bomb crews needed clear weather to successfully strike targets, and the area's lingering monsoon season often forced the cancellation of U.S. bombing missions, giving the enemy time to repair earlier damage to railroads, bridges and factories that supported the war effort. The North Vietnamese had gotten used to the likelihood that during poor weather—or even darkness—"the big noise is no longer gonna fall from the sky," said Clayton.

"The president wanted (North Vietnamese leader) Ho Chi Mihn brought to the peace table," said Clayton, who had completed his second tour of Vietnam in July 1967. When he returned stateside, he looked forward to spending time with his wife and son. He had no reason to expect that he would be back in Southeast Asia by fall. Soon after resuming his permanent position with the 1st CEVG at Barksdale, though, he was sent to the Pentagon to brief a senior officer about Air Force radar capabilities relating to all-weather bombing in North Vietnam. He told him that accuracy would improve if a particular radar system that allowed technicians to calculate bomb-release points ahead of time for pilots was placed within 150 miles of Hanoi. When Clayton finished his presentation, the colonel asked who he thought should lead such an undertaking.

"I kind of jokingly said, 'You're looking at him,'" he recalled.

The Air Staff, though, took him at his word and appointed him commander of the mission, which was code-named Project Heavy Green. There was one major political and ethical problem for the Americans: the radar equipment would have to be placed in neutral Laos; in fact, negotiations allowing this had started prior to Clayton ever returning from Vietnam that summer. Following the defeat of the French in Vietnam by communist-led Viet Minh forces in 1954, Laos had achieved sovereignty via a peace conference in Geneva, Switzerland. It was declared neutral regarding Vietnam War matters in a second conference there in 1961–62. Still, the U.S. State Department's own record of the 1960s admits that America was heavily involved in Laos, as were the North Vietnamese.

In 1967, sending a large contingent of Americans to Laos to operate equipment to bomb a third country was beyond tricky. The Pentagon and White House believed that the risk of U.S. presence in Laos being discovered was worth it if the mission succeeded in getting North Vietnam to negotiate a peace settlement—and they chose the 1st CEVG to lead the effort. There was no question that the men wouldn't go in uniform. When Clayton began compiling a list of those he wanted on the mission, he immediately thought of Dick Etchberger. Though they had never worked together, for many years they were assigned to different detachments within the 1st CEVG and its predecessor, the 3903rd Radar Bomb Scoring Group. Clayton knew that Etch was thought of highly for his radar skills, self-discipline and leadership. They first met around 1954. Clayton, then a captain, had returned from serving as a B-29 aircraft commander in Korea with orders to join a B-36 unit at Travis Air Force Base in Northern California. The Air Force canceled that assignment and instead sent him to work at nearby McClellan AFB in Sacramento after noticing his records showed that he had attended the electronics officers' course at Keesler Air Force Base in Biloxi, Mississippi.

"(They) decided they needed electronics officers worse than they needed pilots," Clayton said, because the Air Force was surveying and building the Distant Early Warning radar net around North America.

Clayton met Etchberger when the latter was a 21-year-old airman second class attending a radio class at Sacramento Army Depot. The young GI stopped by Clayton's detachment to meet others who had the same duties he did at his post in Salt Lake City, Utah. The officer remembers being immediately impressed with Etchberger, who was only a few years out of high school.

"Just his attitude, the way he presented himself, the way he dressed—which was secondary to how hard he worked and how serious he was about his business. It all came to my attention and I knew right then, 'Now here's somebody that we want to hang onto.' And I passed that on up the line," said Clayton.

Because the radar bomb scoring career field was small, Clayton was able to keep track of Etchberger's ascent through the enlisted ranks from afar. Wherever he went within the organization, Etchberger impressed his superiors and was promoted rapidly. So in 1967, when

7

Clayton wanted to bring the most talented radar men with him to Southeast Asia, he invited Etchberger to participate. He didn't get everyone he wanted, battling with his group commander over whom he could take.

"I had been in the organization, of course, since the second battle of Manassas," he said, jokingly referring to the Civil War battle of 1862, "and I knew all (of) the good people and where they were hidden. I had this carte blanche from the Air Force saying, 'Give this guy anything he wants.'"

His superior balked at that, though, saying that he had an organization to run with more to do than one mission in Laos. He ended up with "some really good people," said Clayton, but had others in mind "that the commander just would not turn loose." Staff Sgt. John Daniel was one of the radar men invited to the Project Heavy Green meeting in Louisiana from his post at La Junta, Colorado, with Detachment 1 of the 1st CEVG. He traveled south to the gathering with a co-worker, Staff Sgt. Don Worley.

"(It) kind of made you wonder why you were there as an individual: 'Hell, am I that good? I didn't know that,'" said Daniel. "I think everybody in that room accepted (the assignment) because we all thought we could do some good, and help the military and keep from losing so many aircraft and so many people."

The men were told in no uncertain terms that the covert assignment could help end the war. Etchberger was up for the challenge after just three months stateside following two years in the Philippines. A surreptitious process existed for the sergeants and officers to go to Southeast Asia in civilian status. Each man was required to separate from the Air Force and become an employee of Lockheed Aircraft Services, which Clayton said "had a long record of running the Air Force's spook business." Their families could not remain living on bases. In fact, the men were told that they could move their loved ones anywhere they wanted in the continental U.S. at the military's expense.

"I said a few words to the tune of, 'It is going to be dangerous but we will leave no one behind,'" said Clayton, "and we all went home."

The men returned to their bases. The married ones told their wives they were heading overseas on a secret mission. The Etchbergers decided to move Kay and their two young sons to Dick's Pennsylvania hometown, where his parents, brother and extended family lived. Their older son, Steven, had recently joined the Air Force and been sent to California as an aircraft mechanic. Before leaving the service, the Project Heavy Green men were technically reassigned to Detachment 1 of the 1043rd Radar Evaluation Squadron at Bolling Air Force Base in Washington, D.C., for administrative purposes.

3

The decision to move Kay and their two youngest sons to Hamburg was a natural one for Dick as he knew he could count on his family to welcome them. Etchbergers have made eastern Pennsylvania home for at least 270 years, though the surname has changed slightly through the centuries. It was Etzesberger, Etsberger, Etzberger and Etschberger before finally becoming Etchberger in the early 1800s. The family history in America predates the existence of the U.S. by perhaps a half-century. Through the years, the families lived agrarian lifestyles as was customary in that area then and remains so now for many people, including those who follow Amish and Mennonite religious traditions of simple existence. Various ancestors are described as tenant farmers and millers in government records. A stone home built in 1785 by Jacob Etschberger and his wife, Esther, still stands today in western Berks County, not far from Hamburg.

Founded in 1837, the unincorporated borough of Hamburg is 70 miles northwest of Philadelphia and 55 miles northeast of the state capital, Harrisburg. New York City is a 2-hour drive east on Interstate 78. Hamburg may be best known today as home to the largest Cabela's hunting, fishing and camping store in the United States. Its population has hovered around 4,000 for decades, and it appears today much the same as it did during Dick Etchberger's lifetime. The architecture in the downtown area is dominated by single-family homes and commercial buildings, constructed from the late 1800s to the mid-20th century. Many homes feature tin roofs and ornate tin ceilings made in town. The area has a long manufacturing history, aided by its location on the Schuykill River, which flows through

Philadelphia and into the Chesapeake Bay. Hamburg's residents built fire trucks, brooms, plowshares and other metal goods, and stitched underwear and silk stockings.

Though Dick spent most of his childhood there, he was born 17 miles to the south in Reading on March 5, 1933, to Donald and Kathryn Etchberger, who met as co-workers at a Hamburg clothing factory. He was the couple's second and final child, four years younger than brother Robert. Both boys shared the same middle name, Loy, their mother's maiden surname. Donald was a Reading native who worked as an apprentice stitcher. He moved to Hamburg as a teen to find a job and was hired as a silk hosiery knitter at Burkey Underwear, where he met his wife, a Hamburg native.

"We didn't appreciate Hamburg—it was a great little town, a little sleepy town (where) everybody knows everybody," said Robert. "I don't remember ever having a house key to the back door. You never went in the front door. The back door was open. You went off to bed and that was it. You didn't worry about it."

In the mid-20th century, Hamburg had two banks, competing men's clothing stores, a handful of women's shops, a department store, two hotels and two five-and-dime stores, one of which—Miller's 5 & 10—played a large role in the lives of Etchberger family members for more than 30 years. The business remains open today selling ice cream, souvenirs, hardware and model train equipment. The Hamburg Public Library, opened in 1904, was one of about 3,000 funded by steel magnate Andrew Carnegie.

"It had more industry than the town could support," said Robert Etchberger. "Consequently, people came from outside to work and that trickled down."

Donald Etchberger, called "Red" because of his hair color as a youth, lost his position as a hosiery knitter after the start of World War II when the federal government confiscated the manufacturer's silk supply to make parachutes.

"My dad was out of a job," said Robert. "There was no unemployment compensation in those days. Now here he was with two boys, a wife and no job. He had these mouths to feed."

Red stumbled into a career in the five-and-dime business by chance. The Etchbergers had just bought a home downtown from businessman George Miller, who had substantial real estate holdings in Hamburg. The couple had lost a home to foreclosure during the Great Depression and were determined not to have that happen again. Miller hired Red and Robert, then 12, to maintain properties he owned, and Mr. Etchberger also worked a 12-hour shift each Saturday at the five-and-dime. A friend of Miller who owned a similar store in a nearby coal-mining region was drafted into World War II and would not take a deferment. Instead, Red—who was declared physically unable to serve in the military—went to Philadelphia for a 2-week course in running a retail operation. He then moved his family to Minersville, Pennsylvania, so he could oversee the man's shop. He did so for three years.

When the store owner returned safely from the war in 1945, the Etchbergers moved back to Hamburg. Robert was then a high school junior and Dick was in seventh grade. Red assumed management of Miller's 5 & 10 because the owner wanted to focus on other business interests. Much of Robert and Dick's time was spent working in the store to support the family. The Etchbergers instilled a strong work ethic in their sons, first by having Robert serve there as a stock boy instead of playing high school sports. Dick performed the same duties at the shop after his brother enlisted in the Navy in 1947.

"My father was a very driven person because he lost a home once, and this was never going to happen to him again," said Robert. "The number one thing in the Etchbergers' life was the five-and-ten. You were reminded—once he got back on his feet and things started to go pretty rosy for him—that the five-and-ten did this."

Dick didn't lack for ways to keep himself busy as a youth in Hamburg. As it winds its way 2,175 miles between Georgia and Maine, the Appalachian Trail runs along the crest of eastern Pennsylvania's Blue Mountain, where a young Dick Etchberger camped with friends in the late 1940s. They hiked, built fires, barbecued hot dogs and shot BB guns, which they traded for .22-caliber rifles as they became young men. They talked long into the night about sports, girls and what the future held for them. It's those trips in the woods that Don Yocom remembers most vividly of the time he spent growing up with Etch, as his friend was called then and throughout his future military career.

"We were interested in the same things," said Yocom, who attended Hamburg High School with Etchberger and was his teammate on its struggling basketball squad.

By his senior year in high school, Dick was rail thin and conventionally handsome with a square jaw and thick shock of dark hair. He was president of the class of 1951, a group of 44 students divided evenly between boys and girls. He was vice president of the literary society, treasurer of the speech club, was on the staff of the school newspaper and sang in a boys' double quartet.

"He was very sincere—that's the kind of guy he was," said June Kline, who was class secretary and co-starred with Etchberger in the senior play. Kline was named the school's maypole queen and almost didn't have a maypole to rule over when Dick and friends removed it as a practical joke. That this anecdote survives 60-plus years later is a testament to how simple small-town life was in Hamburg in the early post-World War II years. School authorities started their investigation of the missing maypole at the Etchberger home as it was only steps away from campus and because the principal, who lived next door to the family, recalled seeing Dick arrive home after dark the night before. He called the young man into his office, and Dick quickly admitted that he took it, fibbing that he had acted alone. The school head told the Etchbergers he would drop the matter if the maypole was returned immediately. Dick retrieved it from where he and Don Yocom had stashed it the night before.

"He took the blame for all," his friend recalled.

During his senior year, Etchberger dated Faye Hillenberger, a junior from nearby Strausstown. They met when he visited the home of her much-older sister to see Faye's nephew, Harvey, a classmate of his. Faye knew who Etchberger was from school, but that was the first time she ever spent any time around him. They were both members of the Hamburg High library club and, after an evening meeting, he asked if he could help her arrange some books on a shelf.

"That was the start of it," she said. "He was conscientious about things and committed (and) responsible. He was sort of unusual in comparison to many others at that time."

They dated each other exclusively, and she became close to his family.

"He had something that is lacking today: he had respect for not only me, but for everything. That was one of the reasons I was attracted to him," she said. "He was kind, considerate, (a) gentleman . . . and (had a close) relationship with his parents, his grandma and his aunt and uncle. He was just a good guy."

He was bright, too, she said, an opinion shared by his brother, who described Dick as having a photographic memory that made it easy for him to succeed in his classes with little noticeable effort.

"No matter what that kid did, he did it well," said Robert. "In high school, I'd be up there in my bedroom busting my butt trying to study and Dick would take a half an hour (to finish his homework) and he'd be downstairs. He'd get As and Bs, and I'd get Bs and Cs. That's my brother."

Dick suffered a head injury late in high school when he collided with another boy while playing a pickup game of sports. He was knocked unconscious and stayed overnight in a Reading hospital for observation. The wound later played a significant role in the direction his military career took.

He and Don Yocom talked about enlisting in the Air Force together, but the latter hesitated so Etchberger went off to basic military training alone in late August 1951, several months after graduating Hamburg High. Yocom joined the same service a year later, working in munitions and special weapons for one enlistment before returning home to Hamburg and becoming foreman at a pump company.

Etchberger completed basic training in October 1951 at Sampson Air Force Base near Seneca Lake, New York. His girlfriend and his parents visited him there before he headed to Keesler Air Force Base in Biloxi, Mississippi, to attend an electronics fundamentals course. Dick asked Faye if she still felt the same way about him as she had before he left home. She said she did. He confirmed his love for her and asked her to marry him when he came home at Christmas from a break during his studies in the South. Then a high school senior, she accepted and the two remained engaged while the young airman completed the class and a subsequent one in radar bomb scoring, also at Keesler.

During this time, Etch applied for an Air Force program in which GIs with fewer than two years of college education could train to be pilots. He qualified for it in April 1952 as an airman third class and took the aircrew classification battery exam that August at Moody Air Force Base, Georgia. While waiting for an air cadet's slot, he graduated from the radar class in October 1952, having been promoted to airman second class two months earlier. A black-and-white class photo shows nine young airmen in their dress khakis with their ties tucked inside their shirt buttons so only the top portion is visible, as was custom then. A classmate in the center of the front row holds a mock bomb and a wooden sign with the class name and number on it. All of the young men are thin, but none more so than Etchberger, who stood 5-foot-7 and weighed 130 pounds.

It's uncertain what he did in the months after completing these courses at Keesler AFB, but a letter to the commanding general of the installation shows that Etchberger was not eligible for overseas assignment or other training while awaiting assignment to a flying class. He was in limbo and was likely assigned menial tasks to occupy his time. This is called being in "casual" status, and many GIs have experienced it for short periods while waiting for a class start date. They might mow lawns, paint, clean buildings or possibly even pull some low-level guard duty. Etch returned home quite often during this time as records show he took more than 30 days of leave from December 1952 to May 1953.

He entered pilot training June 1, 1953, at Spence Air Force Base in Moultrie, Georgia. Robert Etchberger, who was then finishing up his Navy commitment near Washington, D.C., remembers a bit about Dick's time in the aviation cadet program, but most of the information the family has is detailed in Air Force records they maintain. One thing that's certain is Etchberger and his classmates quickly took to the air. By late July 1953, he had amassed nearly 17 flying hours and 100 landings in the two-seat, single-engine Piper PA-18 Super Cub— about half of it solo time—and four-plus hours and five landings in the North American T-6 Texas, a single-engine advanced trainer aircraft that he flew with an instructor. Etch was a good student. His highest score was in the navigation portion of instruction, while he was below average in flight instruments. He was average in all other aspects of pilot training, though his leadership aptitude and military conduct grades were excellent. However, an in-air incident threatened his future as an aviator.

On July 29, 1953, Airman Cadet Etchberger was seen by a physician at the Spence AFB dispensary following what a report describes as an "episode of emotional instability while flying." After 30 minutes of flying, an instructor demonstrated a stall and, during it, Etchberger began to cry and threw up his hands. The physician learned about the head injury the young man suffered prior to joining the military. Etchberger told this doctor he had been tested at the hospital during his overnight stay as a teen and was told he had a "slight case of epilepsy." Etchberger disclosed the injury to the Air Force upon enlisting, records show. Dick saw an Air Force neurologist who determined that he had suffered two fainting spells prior to his enlistment. The young airman then met a medical board of officers to discuss what had happened in the air. Etchberger told the panel he was anxious to get into the T-6 following a ride in one during which an instructor demonstrated what acrobatics would feel like.

"Then one day, all of a sudden, I had no coordination. It worried me and . . . it just got the best of me. I had been nervous or maybe reluctant before," he said. "It just built up in me and, one day, it broke me."

Etchberger said the instructor was very helpful in the situation. Still, he made it clear that it was he, not the instructor, who had pulled the aircraft out of the stall. An officer asked if he knew his physical deficiency was a disqualifier for pilot training when he applied for it.

"I was not absolute, but I had a good idea it would be," he said. "They asked me if I had ever had a head injury and I said, 'Yes' and just beat around the bush about it more or less . . . I wanted to fly, sir." He still wanted to fly, in fact, but not at the expense of his own life or that of someone else, he said.

Following the medical board meeting, the panel physically disqualified Etchberger from the flying course. This must have been quite a blow to a young man so accustomed to success in his life. The panel also declined to recommend him for training leading to an officer's commission or other aeronautical rating. Etchberger, then a 20-year-old airman second class, returned to the radar bomb scoring career field nearly a year after completing his class in it. He was assigned to the Phoenix, Arizona, detachment of the 3933rd Radar Bombardment Scoring Squadron at March Air Force Base, California, which itself was subordinate to the 1st Radar Bombardment Scoring Group at Carswell Air Force Base in Fort Worth, Texas.

The overall group consisted of 1,200 to 1,500 people throughout the mid- to late-1950s, the number fluctuating as its mission changed. It was a global organization with three squadrons and 30 detachments, each of which had 30 to 50 people whose mission was to score simulated and live bomb runs and conduct electronic countermeasure training for aircrews assigned to the Strategic Air Command, which had its headquarters near Omaha, Nebraska. They were trying various methods of electronic countermeasures to defend themselves against ground offenses, said Harold A. "Hal" Strack, who commanded the radar bomb scoring group as a colonel for three years in the 1950s.

In addition to the radar bomb scoring squadron at March AFB, there was one at Turner AFB, Georgia, and another located jointly with the group headquarters in Fort Worth. Each had about 10 detachments, six of which were overseas. Each of these sub-units usually had three officers in charge. Some were electronics experts. Many were navigators or pilots. Some were ground officers. Others were a combination of these things. The officer cadre included warrant officers, which the Air Force stopped appointing in 1959 after adding the senior master sergeant and chief master sergeant ranks to the top of the enlisted corps.

"We used these people both to operate the radar and maintain it," said Strack, who flew 72 combat missions as a navigator in World War II and Korea. "We did that because (our) people were of a little higher type. They were pretty good at operating the equipment during scoring as well as maintaining it."

Typically, a unit would get an airman fresh out of training at Keesler AFB and help him become proficient in radar tracking and scoring. Over time, the more experienced men would train him in maintenance of the equipment. During his time in Phoenix, Etchberger broke his engagement to Faye Hillenberger in a letter. She was devastated.

"I think he just wanted to concentrate on his career in the service and wanted out of this other commitment," she said. "He wasn't ready yet, I guess. You grow up after a while. You get out of school and, you know, you think differently."

Faye thinks that Etchberger was devastated himself—by failing the pilot training course, but he never talked to her about it or the head injury that precipitated it.

"He just didn't share things with me that I've found out since, but he just sort of kept from me. I don't know if he thought it would upset me or what," said Hillenberger. "I'm wondering if that didn't change his mind about different things. He wasn't going to be able to do what he planned to do. I know he had to get into (another Air Force career), and he was devoted to doing well in the service. I knew that. He had plans."

Despite the end of their engagement, the two continued to date when he came home on leave, but she noticed a change in him. The relationship, she said, "just sort of . . . faded away," and she later married and raised four children with a man who ran his own coal-trucking business.

This period of Etchberger's career remains murky as the family lacks many records from this time. One thing is clear: he wasn't in Arizona long. In 1954, Etchberger was reassigned to a related detachment at the municipal airport in Salt Lake City, Utah. He received the Air Force Good Conduct Medal August 30, 1954, at his three-year service point and was promoted to airman first class just over a month later. Etchberger left the service after his four-year commitment ended in August 1955 and returned to Hamburg. That fall, he saw Faye and met her fiancé at the wedding of her nephew, Etchberger's high school pal.

His break from the military was short. Just 10 weeks after separating from the Air Force, he re-enlisted for six more years and returned to his former outfit in Salt Lake City. His renewed commitment to the Air Force seems to have lit a fire under him. On February 1, 1956, he was promoted to staff sergeant, the lowest of the noncommissioned officer ranks, a point where an airman begins to transition from follower to leader. He soon caught the attention of Hal Strack, the new commander at group headquarters in Texas. The colonel had heard good things about Etch from Maj. Dick Severin, the Utah detachment commander. Severin believed the young man had great potential and soon convinced Strack to promote him again.

"(He said) I believe that if we showed confidence in him and promoted him that it would ultimately turn out to be a very, very good decision and wise move," said Strack, and it was. "Etch took off like a roman candle. He just became a blazing light of 'do-goodism.'"

Strack promoted him to technical sergeant June 1, 1957, meaning Etchberger spent only 16 months in the E-5 pay grade. These days, most

Air Force NCOs selected for promotion to E-6 have been staff sergeants more than 5½ years and been in the service nearly 11 years. Etchberger was in less than six when he made E-6. At this point, Etchberger was a talented radar bomb scoring technician, a crack maintenance man and a ramrod-straight GI who looked impeccable in his Air Force uniform. He had found a long-term home with the 1st Radar Bomb Scoring Group, and the fit would prove to be mutually beneficial. After his short break in service, Etchberger spent the next 12 years soaring through the enlisted ranks, his pay increasing with his responsibilities.

"There were others like him, but he's one of the outstanding examples," said Strack, who retired as a brigadier general in 1974. "He was one of the best we had, period, among a lot of really, really very good folks."

4

Sending undercover U.S. airmen into a neutral country was more of a diplomatic and political challenge than a military one. It took weeks of cajoling by William H. Sullivan, the American ambassador to Laos, before Prince Souvanna Phouma, the Lao premier, approved of Project Heavy Green, which was in clear violation of the Geneva Accords of 1962. Then serving as the nation's head of state for the fourth time, Souvanna, 66, was previously the country's ambassador to France, where he had attended universities in Paris and Grenoble. French-educated descendants of the royal families held the most political power in Laos 14 years after the nation had gained its independence after a half-century of European rule. The three primary political factions corresponded to categories of the coalition government established in 1962—neutralists, rightists and communists.

Souvanna headed a country of 2 million people diverse in ethnic origin. A CIA report produced in 1967 said at least two-thirds of the population belonged to the Tai cultural populace, including the Lao and Tai tribal groups. The Lao were the politically dominant group, and Lao was the official language. Indigenous minority groups included about 350,000 Lao Theung or mountain people; perhaps 100,000 Meo; 25,000 to 50,000 Yao; and 15,000 to 25,000 various Tibeto-Burman peoples. In addition, there were about 35,000 Vietnamese and as many as 60,000 Chinese. The report describes Souvanna as actively cooperating with the conservative faction in the government and taking a firmer approach to the country's communists after having been more hopeful of reaching an agreement with them in the early 1960s. In a memo to help the White House prepare for a 1967 visit by Souvanna, Ambassador Sullivan described the premier as "at heart a hawk, in private conversation he will make this clear. Publicly, he is, of course, bound by his status of neutrality."

Remarkably, a major threat to Souvanna's rule was from his half-brother, Prince Souphanouvong, who led the Pathet Lao ("Land of Laos") communist organization in fighting against the government, a neutralist-rightist coalition. The CIA estimated that the North Vietnamese Army had 16,000 troops in Laos, 3,000 of which were advisers to the less-capable Pathet Lao. In spite of the international commitment for Laos' impartiality regarding the Vietnam War, Souvanna turned to the West for assistance in countering a communist offensive in 1963. He formally called on the United States to increase its military assistance, a request allowed in the Geneva agreements, which permitted the introduction of "such quantities of conventional armaments as the Royal Government of Laos may consider necessary for the national defense of Laos." U.S. aid was a key factor in preventing further communist gains, but it also aroused suspicions about America's support for a neutral policy in Laos. Still, the United States, the United Kingdom and France did not want to shatter the façade of the Geneva agreements. The CIA produced a 52-page intelligence memorandum, *Laos, The Divided Nation*, in June 1967 just as Washington was pitching its idea for a radar site in the northern part of the country to help its war effort in North Vietnam. The agency's director of economic research, William N. Morell Jr., shared the report in early July with the White House and National Security Council. It acknowledged that the country was in "an uneasy stalemate" between the kingdom and communists that would likely last until the war in neighboring Vietnam was settled.

"The Communists are reluctant to attempt large-scale military actions because of North Vietnam's preoccupation with its own war, the threat of U.S. intervention and the strength of U.S./Lao air and guerilla forces," the report reads. "Their strategy for the present is to hold the eastern corridor of Laos that gives Hanoi an infiltration route to South Vietnam. Souvanna and the Lao Army cannot drive the insurgents out of Laos as long as they are supported by North Vietnam."

Communists held about half of Laos with the direct support of North Vietnamese troops. But the main population and agricultural centers were in areas controlled by the government in the capital,

Vientiane, in the midpoint of the landlocked country, which has a similar shape to that of Italy and wraps around much of Thailand to the west. The standard of living in Laos was possibly the lowest in Asia, and the literacy rate was just 15 percent. Life expectancy was only 30 years, the average year's earnings were under $100 and the country imported 32 times more goods than it exported. The Lao economy was a mixture of primitive agriculture, a business war effort and foreign trade in gold and opium. The economy was too weak to support either the communist insurgency or the defense against it, and both sides were being propped up by substantial foreign aid. Since 1950, the United States had supplied $500 million in diplomatic assistance and $300 million of military assistance, including most of the army's equipment, its logistics system and even some of its food. China and North Vietnam had furnished military equipment and supplies of unknown value to the communists in Laos. Government forces in Laos totaled nearly 100,000 troops, including 1,150 in its air force, which had about 40 small combat planes. The opposing communists had 40,000 Laotian troops and 16,000 from the North Vietnamese Army, but no aircraft. The capabilities of the two forces were determined more by external support available to them than by their own strength.

The job of convincing Souvanna to let American GIs operate a radar-guided bomb system in Laos was left mainly to Ambassador Sullivan acting on direction of the White House and State Department with input from the Pentagon. His boss, Secretary of State Dean Rusk, had been the top U.S. diplomat for six years and believed that the military requirement in this case justified accepting potential political liabilities. On May 6, 1967, Sullivan discussed the need for improved radar capability with Souvanna. Washington suggested that the ambassador not make a specific request for authority to install equipment, but rather present the proposal as an idea the United States was considering. Souvanna, an engineer for the government before he went into politics, asked whether the radar, which would be designed to improve U.S. bombing destruction of North Vietnam, could also function to detect violations of Lao air space. It could, but Project Heavy Green members don't believe it ever was. The system had an effective range of about 200 miles and was an extremely sophisticated navigational device that U.S. aircrews would use for precision bombing of targets even at night and in inclement weather. It would be the first of its kind in Laos, though there were already two each in Thailand and South Vietnam. This ground-directed bombing, as it was called, allowed small teams of men to lock onto an aircraft and guide it to a predetermined release point. It was much more accurate than standard equipment in planes. The Americans had already determined that they wanted to install it atop a 5,800-foot mountain, Phou Pha Thi, in Houaphanh Province in far northern Laos just 12 miles from North Vietnam. The peak was well known to them as it was already home to an air navigation beacon and a dirt landing strip used by the CIA, which had an extensive network of primitive runways throughout northern Laos for use by its Air America and Contintental Air Services Inc. This one, called Lima Site 85, was 140 miles from Hanoi. Phou Pha Thi had served for some time as a major base for guerilla operations. In mid-1967, about 700 Meo irregulars were based there to carry out forays into enemy territory as well as man a defensive perimeter on the border of North Vietnam. Souvanna suggested that the equipment be located at Lima Site 50 atop a mountain in Khoueng Houaphan province east of Site 85, but it was never really considered by the Americans as it would result in about 60 miles of derogation of the system's effectiveness.

"Since all (of) our discussion was conducted in the subjunctive, I cannot give you a precise fix on his probable reaction to a specific request," Sullivan reported to his superiors after the early May meeting with Souvanna where the ambassador initially brought up the radar proposal. "However, I would estimate 70-30 that he would permit installation in North Laos, and only 50-50 that he would buy Site 85."

Sullivan described the premier's mood in a follow-up meeting as cautious, but generally positive. He was concerned about the exposed nature of Phou Pha Thi as it had little vegetation to hide equipment and men. The Americans didn't budge. Taking into account technical aspects and security, it remained Washington's judgment that Lima Site 85 was the only feasible location. Soon, all that really remained to discuss was how the governments would respond publicly if the presence of the radar station and men was discovered. Souvanna said his support of such a radar mission would have to officially be done "without his knowledge," meaning that, if it was exposed, he would deny all awareness of the installation and say the Americans had done it on their own.

He also insisted that technicians be in civilian status with appropriate documentation and that explosives be affixed to equipment to accomplish emergency destruction if necessary. The United States agreed to the latter two points immediately. Undercover Air Force personnel clothed and documented as civilians would operate the facility. How to handle partial or full disclosure of the site took some more finessing on the ambassador's part. Washington requested that Souvanna agree to hold off making any comment on violation of the Geneva Accords until the nature of any disclosure was precisely known and could be discussed. The Americans hoped that Souvanna would not give status of fact to an unconfirmed report. If the United States declined to comment but the premier did, it would be in reaction to a leak, to unsubstantiated charges from the communists or even to statements attributed to U.S. prisoners if the site should be overrun.

"There would be (an) important distinction between his saying 'I have no knowledge of any such facility in Laos' and his saying 'I did not know it was there,'" Washington-based foreign service officer W.C. Hamilton wrote to Sullivan in Vientiane. "We on our part would stop short of 'admitting that we put it there without his knowledge' and of (the U.S. government) 'taking the rap entirely' though we would not waffle any of the blame off on (the Royal Lao Government)."

Souvanna suggested that he might acknowledge the American navigation beacon on the mountain to hopefully satisfy any questioners. Sullivan's counterparts in Washington had thought of the same idea.

"We cannot agree to take on (the) burden of lying to cover Souvanna without even use of a plausible cover story involving navigational aids," the State Department told the ambassador. "This would be politically unacceptable here and would also encourage Souvanna to demand similar arrangements for future U.S. activities in Laos."

Sullivan questioned the wisdom of this proposal, stating flatly, "there is something askew in this response. All that Washington spokesmen would have to do in case Souvanna alleges our unilateral action is to remain silent or to say 'no comment.' In order to give out a prefabricated 'cover story,' spokesmen would have to engage in some rather complex and compounded lying presumably to protect (the U.S. government) while at same time, apparently, alleging that Souvanna is a liar for denying knowledge of our action."

The U.S. decision to move forward with the mission was announced to Sullivan in a June 29 telegram from W.C. Hamilton before the nations had agreed on a response plan in the event of Project Heavy Green's discovery.

"In light of the contradiction between Souvanna's desire for reassurances on specific points and his wish not to know what the (United States) was doing, State would leave to (your) judgment how best to bring him to awareness that we have taken his concerns (which we share) fully into account in reaching decision to proceed," the cable read.

The same State Department communiqué gave the Joint Chiefs of Staff approval to begin installing the radar equipment at Phou Pha Thi, subject to coordination with the U.S. embassy 400 miles southwest of the mountain. Discussion continued for another week between Washington and Vientiane over exactly what would be said in case of different levels of exposure of the operation. The cables show Sullivan's penchant for flowery discourse.

"If we are really caught flat-footed and have no deniable dodges, Souvanna has to know (and I want to know) that his condition will be accepted and respected," Sullivan wrote in one message to Washington. "The (United States) will take the rap entirely. In short, please assure me that all the little George Washingtons will bury their hatchets and not try to shake the cherry tree if the fruit hits the fan."

In another, as the two parties neared agreement on remaining details, Sullivan said, "This should bring all of us angels together on the head of the same pin."

The ambassador explained that Souvanna wanted to know everything about the plan, but he also desired assurance that the United States would not contradict his position that the bomb-related radar equipment was installed without his knowledge. In case of partial disclosure, Sullivan believed that acceptable contingency guidance could be worked out between Souvanna and the embassy at that time.

"In short, he will do the lying," Sullivan said. "He merely wants assurance that you will let him, in that extreme, lie in peace and not contradict him. It seems to me that this is not very much for him to ask and also not very much for us to grant."

In case of total disclosure, the question of citing the United States for a violation of the Geneva Accords would become academic,

Sullivan said, because such a statement and America's own admission "will constitute citation of guilt." Souvanna finally accepted Washington's proposed disclosure postures July 6, 1967. The ambassador assured the premier that all U.S. Air Force markings would be removed from equipment and that measures would be taken to camouflage it against detection from the air. Scrambled transmissions would be used to relay target coordinates from the Project Heavy Green crew to Airborne Warning and Control System aircraft over the Gulf of Tonkin, which would then instantly pass on the information to aircrews on bombing runs to North Vietnam.

Scheduling of the actual installation of equipment was left to the joint 7th Air Force/13th Air Force at Tan Son Nhut Air Base in South Vietnam and the embassy's air attaché in Vientiane. Sullivan requested assurance that information on the installation would be held on the closest need-to-know basis and that all efforts would be made to avoid indications of its location on maps, charts or instructions. He suggested that aircrews should function without actually knowing the exact location of the radar station to prevent them from becoming a source of compromising information should they be captured.

5

I t may been have been the Summer of Love elsewhere in the United States with the Hippie movement galvanizing in San Francisco and other large American cities, but the midpoint of 1967 was anything but that for President Johnson, who was challenged by riots in major American cities and concerned that the country was losing its stomach for fighting the war in Vietnam. American military advisers had been in Vietnam since 1961, while Johnson ordered the first U.S. combat troops there in March 1965. By summer 1967, more than 400,000 Americans were in Southeast Asia.

Fretting that the United States was employing the correct—or even an effective—bombing strategy in Southeast Asia, Johnson consulted with his cabinet and other advisers continually throughout July, August and September. Meeting transcripts show that the men often failed to reach a consensus on what should be done. Even Secretary of Defense Robert McNamara disagreed with much of the advice given by the Joint Chiefs of Staff and military commanders on the ground in Southeast Asia. Johnson, of course, had the ultimate decision. He was in a talkative mood with the press all summer and into the fall, meeting for a series of private interviews in which he expressed hope that the United States could pressure Ho Chi Minh to negotiate an end to the fighting. Washington had instituted bombing pauses to encourage this. They didn't work, and a frustrated Johnson Administration resumed the attacks.

On July 12, less than a week after Lao Premier Souvanna Phouma approved of Project Heavy Green, the president met with McNamara, who was just back from a trip to Vietnam with Under Secretary of

State Nicholas Katzenbach. The defense secretary told the president that military operations were proceeding well, and information on the scene was better than press reports at home indicated. International reporters in Vietnam were "in a very bad mood," he said, and viewed upcoming elections in South Vietnam with uncertainty as they doubted the government could be politically stabilized.

"They are cynical, skeptical and think we have a military stalemate. There is no military stalemate. There is reason to expect significant military losses by the Vietcong in the coming months," the defense secretary said.

McNamara reported that morale among American forces was high and that Gen. William Westmoreland, U.S. military commander in South Vietnam, wanted 100,000 more troops. As to the bombing policy, commanders wanted no restrictions on targets and asked Washington to intensify the attacks. The secretary said he didn't agree with the military's assessment that it had seen improved bombing results since his last trip.

"We have destroyed more, but what we destroyed has less effect on the war effort in the South," he told the president.

Damage to rail lines didn't slow deliveries as much as was hoped because the system's scope was greater than needed by the enemy. U.S. forces had wiped out about 80 percent of North Vietnam's power capacity, but the outcome was dulled by the availability of mobile generators. While air operations had increased the cost to the communists of moving supplies, they had not reduced the flow of them. Air commanders in Southeast Asia wanted to lower existing restrictions around Hanoi and the major harbor city of Haiphong, 55 miles from the capital. They recommended attacking shipping ports and the North's industrial base. U.S. Army Gen. Earle Wheeler, chairman of the Joint Chiefs, acknowledged that the military disagreed with McNamara's bombing advice and assessment, saying that U.S. forces in Southeast Asia had enjoyed an unbroken series of military successes. He recommended bombing restrictions around Hanoi be reduced to a circle of 10 miles and to just four miles in Haiphong. He proposed no attacks on shipping.

"The (United States) and (our) allies should continue maximum pressure," Wheeler said. "The method is unrelenting pressure."

Clark Clifford, chairman of the president's Foreign Intelligence Advisory Board, said public sentiment was that the war couldn't be won. McNamara disagreed, saying that he felt "for the first time" that the United States would win the war if it followed the current tack. President Johnson wasn't so sure. Katzenbach, the number two man at State, said U.S. and allied forces could win the war depending on the performance of the government in South Vietnam. He largely agreed with General Wheeler's bombing advice for Hanoi and Haiphong, adding that he didn't favor another pause in bombing without the North's leaders indicating what they would do in return.

Johnson met July 18 with McNamara, Secretary of State Dean Rusk, National Security Adviser Walt Rostow and his predecessor, McGeorge Bundy, then head of the Ford Foundation, to review 129 targets recommended by Navy Adm. Ulysses S. Grant Sharp Jr., commander in chief of U.S. Pacific Command based in Hawaii. Some were within a 25-mile buffer zone along the country's border with China. McNamara said the targets were largely unimportant, and many were within the still off-limits rings around Hanoi and Haiphong. He predicted a very strong potential for civilian casualties if they were struck. Targets near the center of Hanoi weren't worth the loss of a single U.S. plane or pilot, the defense secretary said. If the proposed Haiphong targets were bombed, ships would be hit, something the administration hoped to avoid.

"Mr. President, your responsibility is to the people of this country," said McNamara. "Whatever you feel we must do, let's do it."

Johnson met July 25 with Senate committee chairmen, including Sen. J. William Fulbright of Arkansas, a war critic who believed that the effects of Vietnam were hurting the budget and foreign relations. The president accused him of having a blind spot on the conflict.

"You say 'Don't bomb North Vietnam' on just about everything. I don't have the simple solution you have. We haven't delivered Ho yet. Everything which has been proposed to Ho has been rejected," Johnson said. "As far as stopping the bombing in North Vietnam, I am not going to tell our men in the field to put their right hands behind their backs and fight only with their left. Bombing North Vietnam gives protection to U.S. ground troops in South Vietnam."

The president told the senators that their chamber had the option of repealing the resolution under which America was in Vietnam.

"You can tell the troops to come home. You can tell General Westmoreland that he doesn't know what he is doing," he said.

Johnson met August 8 with McNamara, Katzenbach, Rostow, White House press secretary George Christian and Joe Califano, the president's special assistant, to hear McNamara present the latest bombing recommendations from the Joint Chiefs of Staff. Military leaders wanted to bomb a thermal power plant, a bridge near a populated area in the capital and 10 targets in the buffer zone along North Vietnam's border with China. They still wanted Washington to lift restrictions on hitting Hanoi and Haiphong. McNamara had spoken to Rusk prior to the meeting, and the secretary of state had rejected all of the proposals except for striking the power plant. Katzenbach, Rusk's deputy, said he had no objections to it either, and the president approved the target. Rostow also supported it and suggested hitting bridges, transportation links within the areas then off-limits and attacking a rail line.

Johnson also permitted hitting targets at least eight miles from China, which were primarily transfer points in transportation lines, and directed McNamara to emphasize to General Wheeler the caution which should be emphasized by pilots to ensure they didn't go over the border. McNamara told the president that he favored no additional action around Hanoi or Haiphong because the possibility of civilian casualties could hamper negotiations with the North as well as compound problems with anti-war "doves" in America. Johnson said an increase in recent bombing didn't appear to be enough to win the war. McNamara believed hitting the approved targets wouldn't necessarily mean victory for the United States. He disputed the Joint Chiefs' claim that hitting the Hanoi bridge would result in few civilian deaths, instead projecting that at least 100 would die. The president directed Katzenbach to study maps of the area and report back to him for a judgment. Johnson was willing to seriously consider taking out the bridge if it was deemed essential to transportation.

"We have got to do something to win," he said. "We aren't doing much now."

McNamara had earlier told the men that military commanders in Vietnam were interested in "free bombing." Katzenbach said he would support lifting Hanoi and Haiphong restrictions if pilots were directed toward targets to hit rather than having authority to strike anything at will. Bombing alone "isn't going to be the magic," said Katzenbach. The combination of strong ground action in the South and good bombing in the North was needed for progress. "Constant pressure adds up," he said.

The president was hopeful for negotiations with the North, but said he saw no need to decrease bombing.

"The moment they are willing, we certainly are ready to sit down. We will discontinue all bombing . . . if we know they will not take advantage of it, but we will not quit until we have their assurance," he said.

A week later, at an August 16 meeting primarily of the same men along with CIA Director Richard Helms, Rusk said the administration needed to clarify its bombing strategy. Johnson said he saw it in the short term as destroying all that the United States could without involving China or the Soviet Union. Rusk was particularly concerned about going after targets along the Chinese border.

"The larger the number of sorties in there, the higher the chances are of mistakes. There appears to be no ascertainable connection between some of these targets and winning the war," he said. "We are trying to wage (it) without enlarging it and without causing the Soviets or the Chinese to give us problems in Berlin or Korea. I have no reservations except on these targets."

The president said the United States needed to hit the least dangerous and most productive targets as the American public wouldn't stay with them unless they destroyed all that they could. At a previous meeting, he had shared a letter from an Arizona citizen who said Americans believed that the civilian heads of government had ignored the advice of the military.

"I would like to be able to say that we have hit six out of every seven targets requested. I think we should get every target as quickly as we can," he said.

Johnson said he had decided to not hit Haiphong harbor and Hanoi yet out of concerns for ships and civilians, respectively, and that he was apprehensive about targets close to the China border "but we have got to put more pressure on," he said.

McNamara said he could get the president 20 more targets to consider. Secretary of State Rusk asked the defense secretary to space airstrikes apart as several attacks on the same day resulted in charges of escalation that may not be in best U.S. interests. Rusk expressed reservations about the significance of the targets.

"It's a question of what do you ask a man to die for?" he asked. "Some of these targets aren't worth the men lost."

McNamara said the Joint Chiefs of Staff recommended a strike on Phuc Yen air base where Soviet-built MiG aircraft were stationed about 20 miles northwest of the capital. They also wanted to restrike targets previously hit inside the 10-mile radius of Hanoi and pursue 25 authorized targets that had yet to be hit. Bombing Phuc Yen was discussed in greater detail in a meeting the president had August 24, the week of his 59th birthday, with Rusk, McNamara, Deputy Secretary of Defense Paul Nitze, Army Chief of Staff Gen. Harold Johnson and Air Force Chief of Staff Gen. John P. McConnell. The base had approximately 11 MiG aircraft at this point, but formerly held more than double that. The others had gone back to China, General Johnson said. McConnell said pilots encountered three types of defensive mechanisms: antiaircraft guns, surface-to-air missiles and MiGs. The United States had lost three aircraft to enemy fighters while downing seven of them.

"Pilots have a growing frustration against our not knocking this MiG base out. If we could, it would permit us to focus on the other defensive systems," said McConnell. "It hurts to see those planes on the runways and not be able to strike them, yet they appear shortly afterwards firing at our planes."

McNamara acknowledged that senior military leaders unanimously recommended hitting Phuc Yen but he was against it as he believed it would cost more pilots than it would save. General McConnell disagreed and said that it would give the men more confidence. The president seemed unsure of what to do, one moment saying that the United States should strike the base and the next contemplating another bombing pause.

"If we believe that we should bomb, then we should hit their bridges, their power plants and other strategic targets outside the ones which we have ruled off-limits," said Johnson. "But I guess a pause won't hurt because the weather is bad anyway. But I do want to get all the targets hit that we dare approve. If they do not talk, we will have to go to more drastic steps. We owe it to our men to do everything we can. We're not."

McNamara said Washington couldn't pause without the military pointing out that there were still targets to hit. Katzenbach advised the president not to step up the bombing before a pause. General Wheeler, the Joint Chiefs chairman, strongly urged the president not to approve a pause, encouraging him to instead open up the 10-mile circle around Hanoi and to let the military hit the Phuc Yen airfield.

"History may make us look silly on this whole thing," the president said. "I think they are playing us for suckers. They have no more intention of talking than we have of surrendering. In my judgment, everything you hit is important. It makes them hurt more. We will give them an opportunity to talk if they will."

Ultimately, Johnson decided to wait to strike Phuc Yen. McNamara was against intensification of bombing, saying it would be harmful toward the American goal of establishing peace talks. Washington had recently written to Hanoi with two options: to meet within two days if the U.S. halted bombing or to talk to negotiator Henry Kissinger, then on the staff at Harvard University, if America held to its current level of strikes. National Security Adviser Rostow said he saw no connection between bombing and negotiations. Katzenbach said continued bombing would not lead to negotiations, telling the president that the administration's softer approach earlier in the year had led to the first U.S. communications with Hanoi in seven months and that the messaging was "less strident" than before.

Bombing discussions continued in the president's Sept. 5 meeting with Rusk, McNamara, Rostow, Christian, Helms and Army Chief of Staff Gen. Harold K. Johnson in place of Wheeler, who was hospitalized after suffering a heart attack. McNamara said the striking of 14 authorized targets had been delayed due to high winds and tropical storms. Four others in the 10-mile radius of Hanoi were held for now. Of 51 remaining targets under consideration, the Joint Chiefs of Staff removed nine after careful examination, and others were pulled because they were previously hit and hadn't yet been repaired. Out of 42 remaining possibilities, McNamara and Rusk were ready to recommend 10, one of which required further photography and another that was in need of fresh intelligence. The thin list of remaining targets would be an adequate number for the next week, McNamara said. The men discussed hitting small petroleum storage sites in Hanoi, but Rusk asked whether destroying these would be so significant as to ask a man to risk his life. McNamara said they weren't and didn't recommend striking them. General Johnson disagreed.

"Men dying is a relative thing," he said. "The effect of the air campaign is a cumulative one, and no one can predict which blow will be the crucial (one) to them. Every blow makes him stretch his resources and, at some point, his resources will not be able to be stretched anymore."

McNamara said remaining targets included four airfields, three ports, five petroleum sites and 19 others, among them seven small targets such as battery, concrete and tire plants. He said there were several important bridges to consider in Haiphong and Hanoi, plus at least five small depot areas. Hitting the bridges and railroads, which were "smack in the middle" of the cities, would be based on their lighter defenses so civilian casualties would be minimized, he said. As for ports, Johnson and his advisers were concerned about hitting vessels from neutral countries. The president suggested giving the military a conditional order that it could strike harbors as long as no foreign ships were present.

"Theater commanders would welcome this kind of latitude," General Johnson said.

McNamara said it might not be feasible to get accurate information from someone on the ground in Haiphong, while Rusk suggested that the order should be that aircraft are not to target any ships, regardless of their country of origin. Cables from this time between the U.S. embassy in Vientiane to State Department headquarters in Washington shed some light on North Vietnam information gleaned from third parties. One such message dated September 6, 1967, from embassy staffer Robert A. Hurwitch details a visit to Hanoi by CBS correspondent David Schoenbrun. The broadcaster/writer was optimistic when he left Vientiane August 22 "that through his lengthy experience in Southeast Asia and long-standing contacts with North Vietnamese leaders, he could somehow bring the war's end closer," but he "returned (September 5) from Hanoi disillusioned and deeply depressed over the prospects for peace."

Schoenbrun met with embassy staffers in Laos for a three-hour debriefing. He said that he was impressed by the "unwavering determination" of North Vietnamese leaders to achieve victory, their "inflexibility" with respect to peace terms and the "remarkable organization and morale" of the "invincible, tireless" North Vietnamese people. Hurwitch wrote that Schoenbrun said during his visits around the country that "his admiration for the energy and morale of the North Vietnamese people knew no bounds," mentioning that he met with North Vietnam Prime Minister Pham Van Dong and even shook hands with Ho Chi Minh during an Independence Day celebration. Schoenbrun said that U.S. bombing had enabled the communists to unite the North Vietnamese people so firmly that he saw "no hope for settlement through negotiations in which the present U.S. administration participated."

On September 29, President Johnson delivered a speech in San Antonio to 2,000 delegates at the National Legislative Conference hosted by the Council of State Governments. In it he offered to cease bombing if Ho Chi Minh would agree to begin serious negotiations for a peaceful settlement of the conflict and if North Vietnam promised not to use the bombing halt as an opportunity to increase its infiltration of troops and supplies into South Vietnam. Johnson tied the hostilities to the early years of World War II by mentioning the lend-lease program in which the United States shipped defense supplies, primarily to Great Britain and the Soviet Union, before entering the war itself against Germany, Italy and Japan.

"For 27 years—since the days of lend-lease—we have sought to strengthen free people against domination by aggressive foreign powers," he said. "But the key to all that we have done is really our own security."

At times of crisis, before asking Americans to fight and die to resist aggression in a foreign land, every president has finally had to answer one question, he said: "Is the aggression a threat not only to the immediate victim, but to the United States of America and to the peace and security of the entire world of which we in America are a very vital part?"

Johnson told the Texas audience of support for America's involvement in the war from leaders of other countries. President Ferdinand Marcos of the Philippines said for the United States to "renounce (its) position of leadership in Asia is to allow the Red Chinese to gobble up all of Asia." Thailand's foreign minister said the American decision "will go down in history as the move that presented the world from having to face another major conflagration." Australia's prime minister said,

"We are there because while communist aggression persists, the whole of Southeast Asia is threatened."

The president acknowledged that he couldn't tell the country with certainty that a communist conquest of South Vietnam would be followed by a subjugation of Southeast Asia as a whole.

"But I do know there are North Vietnamese troops in Laos. I do know that there are North Vietnamese-trained guerillas tonight in northeast Thailand. I do know that there are communist-supported guerilla forces operating in Burma, and a communist coup was barely averted in Indonesia, the fifth largest nation in the world."

Johnson said he didn't know for sure that a Southeast Asia dominated by communist power "would bring a third world war much closer to terrible reality, but all that we have learned in this tragic century strongly suggests to me that it would be so. I am not prepared to gamble on the chance that it is not so. I am convinced that, by seeing this struggle through now, we are greatly reducing the chances of a much larger war. Perhaps a nuclear war. I would rather stand in Vietnam in our time and, by meeting the danger now and facing up to it, thereby reduce the danger for our children and for our grandchildren."

Johnson then turned to the actual fighting of the war, saying that the South Vietnamese, with the help of America and its allies, were making real progress. He said there had been dramatic advancement in the war since America committed to sending more troops there two years earlier.

"The military victory almost within Hanoi's grasp in 1965 has now been denied them," said Johnson. "The grip of the Vietcong on the people is being broken."

The president said his administration and its South Vietnamese allies were prepared to negotiate immediately with North Vietnamese representatives to hopefully end the war.

"I am ready to send a trusted representative of America to any spot on this earth to talk in public or private with a spokesman of Hanoi. We have twice sought to have this issue of Vietnam dealt with by the United Nations and twice Hanoi has refused."

The president said the United States had repeatedly told Hanoi that America was willing to stop all aerial and naval bombardment of

North Vietnam if it would lead promptly to productive discussions, but North Vietnam's leaders had not accepted any of the proposals.

"So it is by Hanoi's choice—and not ours, not the rest of the world's—that the war continues," he said.

Johnson said North Vietnam's leaders hoped that the people of the United States would not see the struggle through to the end, quoting a western diplomat just back from a visit to Hanoi who said the communists "believed their staying power is greater than ours and that they can't lose."

"The premier of North Vietnam said as far back as 1962 (that) 'Americans do not like long, inconclusive war . . . thus we are sure to win in the end,'" said Johnson.

The president believed they were wrong because it was "the common failing of totalitarian regimes that they cannot really understand the nature of our democracy."

"They mistake dissent for disloyalty," Johnson said. "They mistake restlessness for a rejection of policy. They mistake a few committees for a country. They misjudge individual speeches for public policy. They are no better suited to judge the strength and perseverance of America than the Nazi and the Stalinist propagandists were able to judge it. It is a tragedy that they must discover these qualities in the American people and discover them through a bloody war."

Johnson said the price of the efforts had been heavy for the U.S., with 13,500 killed in action and 85,000 wounded, but the price of not having made them at all would have been vastly greater.

"Our goal has been the same in Europe, in Asia, in our own hemisphere. It has been, and it is now, peace. And peace cannot be secured by wishes. Peace cannot be preserved by noble words and pure intentions," said Johnson, who ended his San Antonio remarks by promising that the fight would continue. "Two things we must do. Two things we shall do. First, we must not mislead the enemy. Let him not think that debate and dissent will produce wavering and withdrawal. For I can assure you, they won't. Let him not think that protests will produce surrender. Because they won't. Let him not think that he will wait us out. For he won't."

A few nights later, President Johnson gathered his advisers at the White House to talk about the San Antonio speech. With him were Rusk, McNamara, Rostow, Helms and Christian.

"What I want them to know is that I will stop the bombing and enter negotiations which are prompt and productive," the president said. "We have always assumed that they would not take advantage of the bombing. Let's not let them say that we have retracted our assumption. This proposal may lead them to a meeting, but it may lead me into a trap. I know I will be charged with bad faith if they enter talks then begin firing at us."

McNamara said the United States was making slow progress.

"I have no idea how we can win it in the next 12 months," he said. "We have to do something to increase the support for the war in this country. I know of no better way to do it except by a pause."

Then Johnson dropped a bombshell of his own: he asked these five men what effect there would be on the war if he announced he was not going to run for another term as president the following year. He said he thought it would be advantageous to welcome candidates to share their ideas with the American public.

"You must not go down," said Rusk. "You are the commander-in-chief, and we are in a war. This would have a very serious effect on the country. Hanoi would think they have got it made."

"I don't think you should appear too cute on this," said McNamara, adding that they needn't worry about the continuing flow of money and men. "I do not know about the psychology in the country, the effect on the morale of the men and the effect on Hanoi. I do think that they would not negotiate under any circumstances. They would wait for the 1968 elections."

Johnson said the American public would not support four more years of war.

"I want to get rid of every major target," he said. "Between now and the election, I am going to work my guts out. I would be 61 when I came back in, and I just don't know if I want four more years of this. But I am afraid it would be interpreted as walking out on our men. We are very divisive. We don't have the press, the newspapers or the polls with us, though when I get out into the country it seems different than it is here."

6

ick Etchberger met waitress Catherine Jewel Wilson in 1956 at the Hi Jinks, a Salt Lake City restaurant he frequented. The sergeant, 23, struck up a friendship with Kay, who was five years older than him and had a son from an earlier marriage.

"I really believe it was love at first sight," said her sister, Helen, who also worked at the eatery, as did a third sister, Rose. "You could actually see it from them talking. They met each other (and) next thing you know they were sitting in a booth."

The couple dated for six months before they married in a private civil ceremony January 23, 1957, in Phoenix, where Etchberger had been stationed briefly two years earlier. They honeymooned at the Grand Canyon before returning to Utah to start their life together with Steven, 9.

"Kay never was much for talking about things, but . . . I knew it was going to happen and it did," said Rose. "He was quiet and so neat and nice with her. He was very polite. He was just that kind of guy that you take to and you like."

Steven had no idea his mother was even dating anyone until she introduced Dick to him one day and said they were going to marry. The boy's first concern was what to call his future stepfather. Etchberger alleviated that worry by telling him he could simply call him Dick. The family quickly grew with the birth of son Richard that November. Rose remembers watching the boys when the couple went for dinner and dancing at the Hill Air Force Base Noncommissioned Officers Club.

"Kay was so happy—that makes a difference," she said. "Dick respected people. He respected us. He treated us just like family."

Technical Sergeant Etchberger then got reassignment orders to Morocco in early 1958 and the family shipped off to northwestern Africa, where a third son, Cory, was born in January 1959. Dick was assigned to Detachment 2 of the 12th Radar Bomb Scoring Squadron, working as a shift chief of a bomb scoring crew, evaluating simulated bomb runs made by B-47 Stratojet aircrews stationed in Morocco and Spain. He flourished in the austere environment, leading two staff sergeants and having indirect supervision of 15 airmen. Men of 1st Radar Bomb Scoring Group detachments were used to fending for themselves in areas that were often far from services normally provided at U.S. military bases.

"Those people could do anything," said Col. Jerry Clayton, a 1st RBSG veteran who later commanded Etchberger in Southeast Asia. "They were out in the boondocks and not only did they not have access to GI medical care and commissaries, they didn't have a civil engineer to call when things broke. They literally put things together with their own hands. I've never been as proud of my service as the time I spent in that organization."

Etchberger was rated high on his 1958 performance report by his supervisor, Master Sgt. Harold B. Lebaron, and Detachment Commander Capt. Tom A. Reeves. The latter expected Etchberger to "emerge as one of the strongest NCOs in the Air Force—a top leader as well as an outstanding technician." Lebaron noted that Etchberger had recently passed the entrance examination for Officer Candidate School, taking the battery even though the medical flight panel had rejected him for the same consideration six years earlier because of the head injury he'd suffered as a teen. He earned the detachment's Outstanding NCO Award for 1959. Reeves described him as "bursting with an abundance of nervous energy, whose every thought and notion is directed toward improving the methods of job performance, working conditions or site facilities so that his unit will consistently operate at the optimum level." His 1959 performance report noted his ability to work under pressure. Though he was NCO in charge of operations, Etchberger was a fully qualified maintenance supervisor and could fill the position of maintenance chief at any time, Lebaron said.

"I have never known a more hardworking or capable NCO," Lebaron wrote in a simple statement that was nevertheless high praise from a career enlisted GI. "(He) invariably injects into his subordinates a feeling of intense enthusiasm and a desire to complete the task at hand as proficiently and expediently as possible. He is forceful and demanding in dealing with personnel under his supervision, but he is not overbearing."

While in Africa, Kay Etchberger exchanged frequent letters with her sisters and swapped taped conversations with her in-laws in Pennsylvania. Dick's parents visited them overseas soon after his mother expressed concern upon hearing a recording of her toddler grandson, Rich, speaking French instead of English to a Moroccan woman who helped around the family's home. Steven Wilson remembers the family enjoying their time in the exotic locale, where he and other children rode 40 miles each way by bus to attend an American-run school. He spent lots of time with Rich and Cory, who were his main sources of entertainment because the family did not have a television set.

In summer 1959, Etchberger was reassigned to Bismarck, North Dakota, when his Morocco unit transferred there, becoming Detachment 10 of the 11th Radar Bomb Scoring Squadron. The northern plains would be the family's home for the next six years. Etchberger was a member of the advance party for the move and was appointed NCO in charge of operations and maintenance, serving in a position rated for a sergeant two grades higher than his. Reeves remained his detachment commander in North Dakota. A July 1960 letter from the captain to Etchberger and his parents describes how much his superiors thought of him after his section excelled during an inspection by a team from group headquarters in Texas. His annual written performance reports from this time reinforce these feelings. Electronics officer Capt. William E. Gardiner, his immediate supervisor, said Etchberger led rather than directed and was one of the most eager and versatile NCOs he had encountered. Reeves described Etchberger as the most fully qualified technician and supervisor he had observed and said he shouldered his responsibilities in a truly professional manner.

"In appearance and conduct, he is more like a young commissioned officer recently graduated from an academy than an NCO," Reeves said. "His growth potential as a technician and supervisor is unlimited."

As dedicated as he was to his military career, Etchberger was an involved parent and husband, relatives recall. His sister-in-law, Rose, said he was an excellent father and treated Kay wonderfully.

"He was good to the boys," she said. "He wasn't mean about it. He was a kind-hearted person."

Steven, whose father had died shortly after his parents' divorce, had grown close to Dick in the years since he married Kay. Etchberger never once introduced him as his stepson, always as his son, and treated him as he did the younger boys. That said, Dick expected an orderly home life.

"What he said, went. That was it," Wilson said. "If he said no, you didn't ask twice. There was no discussion. He was that type of person who, when he put his mind to something, it was done. There was no question about it."

The teenager respected Dick's discipline, recalling that he quit cigarettes abruptly after U.S. Surgeon General Dr. Luther L. Terry released an advisory committee's report linking smoking to health dangers.

Kay became pregnant in 1963, and it led to a test of the couple's strength when their daughter, Loy Elizabeth, died at birth. They never spoke about the tragedy with family, not even to Steven, then 16. Dick called Kay's sisters and mother in Utah to let them know of the death and requested that the family not come to visit as it was such a sad time for them. Soon after, Etchberger completed an in-depth course in a new radar system that kept him away from Bismarck for six months. He took over the instruction at one point when it was apparent to him that the assigned instructors were not fully qualified, Captain Reeves noted in a performance review. He continued his climb through the NCO ranks, obtaining promotions to master sergeant and senior master sergeant in 1961 and 1963, respectively. He personally supervised five NCOs who had 30 airmen under them and he graduated with honors in 1962 from the 15th Air Force Senior NCO Academy at March Air Force Base near Riverside, California, which trained him in leadership responsibilities of the service's most-senior sergeants.

During his time in Bismarck, Etchberger served on a Strategic Air Command team of inspectors that traveled on rail cars to rate B-52 Stratofortress crews around the country. The team consisted of 30 people or more on trips of 45 days, said retired Maj. Stan Sliz, who worked with Etchberger in North Dakota and later served with him in Southeast Asia. The train was self-sufficient with communications, supply, food service and more. It would usually have five or six cars: one for radar operations, another for power, a dining car and two for living quarters with desks that doubled as beds. Bomber aircrews from around the world would fly to the train's changing location, performing in-air refueling and flying a low-level bombing route, tripping electronic signals for scoring rather than dropping live ordnance. The inspectors were evaluated themselves as they dealt with aircrew attempts to electronically jam the ground radar systems. Etchberger's professionalism was indicative of everyone in the radar bomb scoring field, Sliz said.

"Everybody was a pro. If you didn't fit, they got rid of you in a year. If they liked you, they found ways to keep you there," he said. "Etch was real sharp. Spit and polish. He was always immaculate. He'd say, 'Captain, sir.' He was well versed in his profession."

In 1963, Etchberger organized an association within his detachment to instruct NCOs in their responsibilities as professional military leaders, customs of the service and to inspire leadership.

"(It) has developed a definite improvement in the effectiveness of the NCO personnel at this detachment," Maj. Donald L. Marks, the detachment commander who succeeded Reeves, wrote in a performance review of the sergeant. "He is the most outstanding NCO leader I have ever known."

On the same report, 11th Radar Bomb Scoring Squadron Commander Lt. Col. Reynold C. Dorman said he saw no limit to Etchberger's potential and recommended that he be integrated into the regular officer force. Subsequent supervisors had the same opinions of him as their predecessors. Marks said Etchberger had the highest degree of professionalism and motivation he had ever known.

"Every task he undertakes is accomplished with outstanding excellence. Every task gets a professional touch," he wrote about him in an assessment.

While the Etchbergers' younger boys started their elementary school education in Bismarck, son Steven attended junior high and high school there, meeting his future wife, Kathy, at a community dance. By the time he graduated in June 1965, the family had been in North Dakota for six years, an eternity by military assignment standards then in place. Dick was ripe for a move, and it came when he drew orders to Clark Air Base outside of Manila in the Philippines. He was approaching the peak of his Air Force career, and the new job gave him his first taste of the growing war in Vietnam.

Two career enlisted airmen who worked with Etchberger at Clark consider him the finest noncommissioned officer with whom they ever served. That's high praise considering the average GI works with hundreds of NCOs and knows thousands in the minimum of 20 years it takes to reach retirement point. The Etchbergers arrived at Clark in June 1965 for a two-year tour. Dick—then a senior master sergeant, the Air Force's second-highest enlisted rank—was assigned to the 608th Tactical Control Squadron, part of the 5th Tactical Control Group at Clark, one of the most important and busy bases in the Pacific and home to 13th Air Force headquarters. Etch arrived there a few months before his eventual supervisor, Chief Master Sgt. Earl Osborne, who had worked in the radar field ever since the word "radar"—short for radio detection and ranging—was classified information in World War II. Etchberger secured his new boss quarters in a section of officer's housing on base where he was to live with his family their entire stay in Philippines. Osborne remembers that Dick had stocked the refrigerator and cupboards before their arrival.

"It was a very thoughtful gesture, more than most people would do," Osborne said.

Another man who still thinks the world of Etchberger is Ed Perrigo, who served under him at Clark Air Base as a technical sergeant.

"Etch was an outstanding NCO. He's the kind of a guy that took care of the people that worked with him and was very sensitive and concerned about people's needs," said Perrigo. "He was an NCO's NCO. I never heard anyone say anything negative about him. They had nothing but praise for him. He was intelligent, industrious, a good worker, a good friend."

The 608th Tactical Control Squadron's primary function was to provide radar support in the Vietnam War effort. Members of the unit would receive radar equipment, assemble and test it, and then a team of up to 75 people—including cooks, supply technicians, truck drivers and others—would install it in either Vietnam or Thailand, and always, Perrigo said, "in the middle of nowhere."

"Once we got them over there, we would put them together, test them and then wait for personnel to come from the (United States) to take over (operating) the radar. Then we'd return to the Philippines and repeat the process," he said. The squadron had an auxiliary mission of evaluating sites for radar placement. Part of the work was air defense—looking for potential enemy bombers—but primarily it was tactical. They linked F-105D Thunderchiefs and new F-4C Phantom II aircraft with refueling tankers and directed aircraft to targets. They also provided technicians if forward-deployed radar units needed something repaired or required a temporary replacement.

"We'd go over there, fix it and then come home," Perrigo said. "We might go one at a time or with a handful of people. We did a lot of that sort of thing. It was a pretty adventurous life. We never knew where we were going to sleep. We never knew from one night to the next where we were going to be. We had to be pretty innovative."

Etchberger and Perrigo deployed together a few times, but Dick primarily served in an administrative capacity at Clark by virtue of his rank. When Perrigo was away, Etchberger checked on his family and always ensured they had fresh drinking water.

"In the Philippines, if you lived off-base, it was not safe to drink the water," Perrigo said. "You had to carry it in five-gallon cans to your home off-station and he would arrange for someone to bring it to my wife on a scooter or a motorcycle. He did that for all of the spouses."

The Etchbergers also lived off-base and grew close to the Osbornes. Their families dined together at the NCO Club and in each other's homes. Osborne, 12 years older than Dick, remembers liking Kay Etchberger.

"She was a real fine person, a strong supporter of Etch," he said. "She backed him 100 percent in his endeavors and took good care of the boys."

Osborne prepared a performance report of Etchberger in May 1966 in which he wrote that his subordinate "is the most outstanding NCO I have known."

"That still stands," Osborne, 93, said in February 2015 by phone from his home in Tucson, Arizona, where he retired from the Air Force in 1974. The glowing report said Etchberger possessed "the extraordinary feature of insuring that all tasks are completely resolved without follow-up from his supervisor" and cited his "positive attitude, resourcefulness, extraordinary efficiency and outstanding professional competence (that) has contributed significantly to the accomplishment of the squadron mission."

Maj. Hugh C. Hale, an endorsing official on the performance review, said Etchberger's "technical ability surpasses that of any individual I have ever known." He also recommended that he be given a direct commission to captain if a proposed limited-duty officer program was enacted.

"This outstanding NCO would be a definite asset to the officer corps," he wrote.

Before ending his tour at Clark, Etchberger received his final promotion. He was upgraded to chief master sergeant on April 1, 1967, shortly before leaving the Philippines for an assignment in Illinois. The rank is achieved by just 1 percent of the enlisted force. Perrigo hated to see Etchberger leave for the United States because he realized how special he was.

"He was just my very good friend. We were like brothers," he said. "He was kind of a special individual to me. You meet scores and scores of men in the service and, after a year or so, you forget their names. But somehow Etch and I were like soul mates."

7

In September 1967, while the Project Heavy Green men busied themselves with moving their families to new homes before heading overseas, Reeves Instrument Corp. of Buffalo, New York, manufactured the radar equipment they would operate in Laos. This was the same company that built the TSQ-81 gear already in use by the 1st Combat Evaluation Group, but the Phou Pha Thi mission required a portable configuration so men in helicopters could bring it to the peak in pieces prior to the team's arrival. Reeves and the Air Force developed this MSQ-77 radar system, which could track a plane within 200 miles. The system had an early computer that continuously calculated the altitude, airspeed, wind drift correction and ground elevation changes, using the ballistics of the particular bombs aboard the aircraft. Based on the computation, a plotting board drew a precision paper map of where a jet was in relation to a target. Radar equipment on fighter-bomber aircraft of the Vietnam-era wasn't nearly as capable as the ground-based system such as the type atop Phou Pha Thi, which required an officer serving as lead radar controller to be in radio communication with the pilot. He would direct him to make minor corrections in his flight path as required and announce the exact moment to drop bombs to ensure they would be on target.

Reeves Instrument Corp. shipped the portable system to Bryan Field, Texas, where a team of Air Force radar technicians and officers who knew nothing about the upcoming Laos mission tested it. They put it together and disassembled it, then repeated the steps, assessing it by directing aircrews to drop live bombs on Madagorda Island on the

Gulf Coast. It worked perfectly, and they shipped it to Southeast Asia for installation atop Phou Pha Thi.

Lt. Col. Bob Seitzberg, who had worked for Clayton at 1st CEVG headquarters in Louisiana, was then assigned to 7th Air Force headquarters at Tan Son Nhut Air Base in South Vietnam. Before the arrival of the Heavy Green men, he was sent up to the mountain with surveying equipment to confirm the location was appropriate for the operation. He determined that it was. A Navy demolition team soon visited it to blast away enough rock to make a level spot for the radar system and living quarters.

The peak's existing landing strip, called Lima Site 85 in CIA parlance, was well known to Air America crews as an aerial resupply point for friendly guerilias. The CIA had trailers for a few men near the runway, and the peak had been home to a navigational beacon for at least two years. Chopper crews and pilots flying Porters, a fixed-wing aircraft capable of short takeoffs and landings, frequented Lima Site 85. The enemy also knew about it. In late 1966 and early 1967, North Vietnamese troop buildup in northern Laos had been observed as a potential threat to several Lima sites. The enemy, in fact, had already attacked Lima Site 36, headquarters of Hmong Gen. Vang Pao's CIA-trained forces 30 miles southwest of Phou Pha Thi.

A team led by Lt. Col. Alan Randall and Chief Master Sgt. Andrew Borne, two longtime members of the Air Force radar bomb scoring career field, assembled the equipment while on temporary duty from 1st CEVG headquarters in Louisiana. Helicopters carried large pieces of equipment from the CIA landing strip to the newly leveled spot a quarter-mile or more away. Smaller ones were brought up a rocky trail by hand. All of this helicopter and explosive activity wasn't lost on unfriendly forces in the valley. They already knew of the CIA men up top and of the Hmong and Thai defensive forces in place protecting them, said Clayton. The radar equipment was housed in rectangular metal trailers placed as an L. The system included a dish that was about eight feet in diameter and sat atop a pedestal on a portion of the trailer containing the controls, cables and the computer. The radio and supplies were in the other section.

While the installation was underway in Laos, the Project Heavy Green men went to Bolling Air Force Base in Washington, D.C., to complete paperwork to cover their tracks in case they were discovered in the neutral country. The sergeants ended their enlistments. The officers resigned their commissions. At the same time, though, the men completed undated forms that said these actions were, in effect, nothing more than clerical errors, simple mistakes ending the military careers of two-dozen career GIs, some of whom had served 15 or even 20 years. This way, if the men died while working undercover for Lockheed, Air Force clerks could process these forms so their families would get survivor benefits from the federal government. Dick Etchberger's sheet asked the Air Force to reflect that he had been on continuous active duty since 1955, when he re-enlisted after the 10-week break in service he had following his first four-year hitch. It was kept in a file in Washington, D.C., with similar paperwork from his teammates. Those who were married brought their wives to Washington to attend a briefing about the project. Afterward, the women were sworn to secrecy.

"We all were just excited and happy," said Ann Sliz, whose husband Stan was selected for the mission and had worked with Etchberger previously in North Dakota. "Really thrilled that our husbands had been chosen."

Also at this time, Pentagon officials dropped a surprise mission on Jerry Clayton, the Heavy Green commander. They needed his men to keep the mountain's existing TACAN flight beacon operational, one in a system of dozens spread throughout Laos, Thailand and South Vietnam that helped allied aircrews navigate the region. This additional task would pose a great challenge to Clayton.

"I couldn't spell 'nav aids' hardly when handed that," he said.

The couples said their farewells to each other in the nation's capital. The women returned to their homes, while their husbands flew to a Lockheed operation in Ontario, California, 40 miles east of Los Angeles, to fill out civilian employment paperwork. The men learned about their salaries and life insurance plans. While a GI policy paid $10,000, their new employer's arrangement was worth seven times that. The men were put on the Lockheed payroll after the Air Force computed the value of a military career, including their medical benefits, and commissary and exchange shopping privileges.

"They threw all that in, plus a little kicker, and that's what we were all paid, according to our pay grade," said Clayton. "We did everything except take lie detector tests. The rest of it, we all did."

While in Southern California, Etchberger had time to visit his stepson, Steven Wilson, then 19, who had enlisted in the Air Force the previous winter and was stationed at Norton Air Force Base in San Bernardino, just 20 miles from the Lockheed operation. Wilson had married his high school sweetheart, Kathy, a month earlier, but Dick was unable to attend the North Dakota ceremony because of all of the tumult caused by his preparations to head overseas. He secured a car and surprised the young couple at their apartment. It was the first time he had seen them since getting the news that he was going to be a grandfather.

Steven had joined his family in moving to the Philippines after graduating high school in 1965, but returned to North Dakota after just a few months to work as a gas station attendant and attend National College of Business in Rapid City, South Dakota, while Kathy completed her senior year of high school. He received a draft notice in 1966, prompting him to visit a recruiter from his stepfather's branch of service. Wilson enlisted and was trained as an aircraft mechanic at Chanute Air Force Base, the same location Dick was reassigned to following his tour in the Philippines. The young airman graduated from his course there in June 1967 just as his parents and brothers arrived home from overseas. The family had one day of overlap at Chanute before Wilson departed for the West Coast. It was the first time all five of them had been together in 20 months.

By the time Etchberger arrived at the Lockheed operation in California, his stepson was working for the 63rd Military Airlift Wing, which was building up a massive new fleet of silver C-141 Starlifter cargo aircraft that constantly shuttled troops, equipment and supplies, to and from the Pacific. Dick took Steve and Kathy to Disneyland amusement park and then to dinner a night or two later. Wilson doesn't remember Dick discussing his upcoming assignment in detail. He certainly didn't mention Laos.

"He might have said he was going to Thailand or something, but not much more than that," Wilson said.

Another thing he didn't reveal was that in accepting the Heavy Green duty, he had struck a deal with the Air Force that Steven wouldn't be deployed to Vietnam while Etchberger was overseas on his one-year mission. The radar men left California on a civilian airliner bound for Hawaii, where they boarded a military transport. They stopped at Clark

Air Base in the Philippines for a few days so some of the men could attend tactical air navigation system training to learn how to maintain the beacon atop Phou Pha Thi. Etchberger stayed with Earl Osborne, his former supervisor, and told him that the men were headed out on a classified mission—"all hush-hush and that they had to wear civilian clothes," recalled Osborne, whose wife fixed dinner one night for Dick and two of his teammates. Etchberger used the couple's car to run some errands and then said goodbye to them, heading for Udorn Air Base, Thailand, with about two dozen other men who made up the Heavy Green team.

Etchberger was back in the Far East just five months after he left the Philippines, but the gap between tours in the region was even shorter for Jerry Clayton. The Heavy Green commander had completed his second Vietnam tour in June 1967 without any expectation that he would be back soon. Instead, he returned to the region just four months later. Upon his arrival, Clayton went to the U.S. Embassy in Vientiane, the Lao capital, to meet with Ambassador William Sullivan. The diplomat told him that the Heavy Green men would have at least 24 hours' notice to abandon the mountain and that the colonel should not worry about security as that was Sullivan's concern.

"Our job was to drop bombs," said Clayton. "(Sullivan) made it clear that, in this case, he was the final authority to order evacuation."

Thailand's Udorn Air Base, 240 miles northeast of Bangkok and 50 miles south of Vientiane, served as Project Heavy Green's administrative headquarters. In fall 1967, the base was a beehive of activity with F-4 Phantom flight operations conducted around the clock by the 432nd Tactical Reconnaissance Wing. Heavy Green's administrative center was set up in Quonset huts adjacent to the flightline and run by Master Sgt. Frank Roura, a senior clerk from a radar bomb scoring detachment in La Junta, Colorado. The base had separate clubs for officers and enlisted men, a theater, a "Class 6" shop selling alcohol, an exchange store and a commissary where GIs could purchase groceries. The base even had a golf course between its runways.

"It was just an ordinary Air Force base, lots of concrete and dirt," said Roura, who had served there previously in 1965-1966. "Nothing about it stood out compared to others. We slept in wooden huts, nothing sumptuous or anything."

The men were divided into two teams of 11. While the first would deploy to the mountain, the second group would remain at Udorn and largely be on their own until it was time for them to head to Laos to relieve the others. Some went in together to rent off-base homes, but the most-senior stayed on-base to oversee things. Udorn was where Clayton and Lt. Col. Bill Blanton, his deputy, would spend most of their time while other men, the actual equipment technicians and radar controllers, rotated to the peak. Etchberger was a no-nonsense man, a master scavenger and a "lead or get out of the way and let me" sort of person, Clayton said. Dick was the senior noncommissioned officer on his squad, and the commander had come to prize his demeanor and military bearing. He was respected by the men above and below him. Because he had spent years as a radar bomb scorer, he could easily fill in for any of the men who operated the radar equipment. When he wasn't on the mountain, Etchberger roomed with Roura, who was amazed at how rapidly the mission came together following the initial meeting in Louisiana.

"It was fantastic. Looking back at it, I am amazed at how quickly it just melded together into an operational unit. Really, it just came out of nowhere," said Roura. "When you think about that—how many men had to move, the equipment—our guys were pretty damned good, I'd say."

Even though none of the Heavy Green men who worked in Laos technically remained in the service, at Udorn they wore Air Force uniforms and still had their military IDs to help maintain secrecy of the mission. The radar men were used to a heavy temporary duty travel schedule and "damn near kept a bag packed," said John Daniel, a board operator on the team as a staff sergeant. Staying put for a year was unusual for them, even if it meant dividing the time between Thailand and Laos.

In Washington, President Johnson waited for a North Vietnamese response to negotiating terms he had proposed in his San Antonio speech a few weeks earlier. He had offered to send Henry Kissinger to meet with their representatives in Paris. Any hope was dashed, though, when the Johnson Administration received Hanoi's discouraging reply:

At the present time, the United States is continuing the escalation of the war in an extremely grave manner. In these conditions, words of peace are only trickery. At a time when the

United States continues the escalation, we can neither receive Mr. Kissinger nor comment on the American views transmitted through this channel. The position of the Government of the Democratic Republic of Vietnam is perfectly clear. It is only when the United States has ceased without condition the bombardments that negotiations can take place.

If the North Vietnamese response had included any hope, the Project Heavy Green men may never have left Udorn. Instead, the first team of radar specialists went to the operation's huts, stripped out of their Air Force uniforms and put on matching dark green civilian work clothes they had purchased in California. They left their military identification cards with Frank Roura, who gave them Lockheed employee credentials to take with them to the mountain. It was about a two-hour helicopter ride from Udorn to Phou Pha Thi. The plan was to have half of the men remain in Thailand on break while the others operated the radar equipment in Laos for a week before switching places. The men soon decided, though, to double the length of time they would stay on the hill because it took so much effort to get them there and back.

Among the first Heavy Green technicians atop the mountain was John Daniel, who saw from the chopper that the peak was nearly devoid of vegetation, but the valley below it was a thick carpet of jungle. Raised on a farm near Springfield, Missouri, Daniel had joined the Air Force in 1959 and completed electronics and radar training the following year. His best friend on the Heavy Green team was Staff Sgt. Don Worley, a co-worker from their radar detachment in La Junta, Colorado, the same one where Roura worked. Daniel also knew Technical Sgt. Patrick Shannon, a fellow Missourian who was stationed in La Junta before being reassigned to a radar site in his home state. This was the second time in Southeast Asia for Daniel, who had helped build a radar site at Bien Wah, South Vietnam, during a temporary assignment in 1965 that also was commanded by Jerry Clayton. As he arrived at the mountain for the first time, Daniel understood the bare minimum of what he and the others would do at Lima Site 85 and nothing of what the CIA did at its portion of the peak.

"We (only) knew we was just going in to operate it, that someone else had gone in and built it," said Daniel. "Fact is, we never seen anyone there. We never seen who it was who we were replacing."

55

The helicopter came to a halt on the landing strip and the men walked uphill to a trailer that served as their living quarters. The radar equipment was placed nearby. Though Clayton commanded the operation from Udorn, he went to the site with the first group of men and visited from time to time to check on things. His first impression was that the peak was "pretty much inaccessible" on the east side due to the steepness of a massive cliff there. The peak was heavily defended on other sides by a complement of Lao natives and Thai forces hired by the CIA. These forces were to hold the mountaintop in the event of an attack, giving the Americans time to blow up the equipment before departing.

John Daniel doesn't recall the team members being too concerned about their safety as they showed up for work the first time. He remembers getting to the peak, turning on the equipment and quickly going to work, perhaps that first day. The men were directed to support bombing runs via a teletype message called a fragmentation order from 7th Air Force/13th Air Force headquarters in South Vietnam. They printed the "frag," which told them the longitude and latitude of a target, but nothing about its nature. They had no idea whether it was a bridge, a train track or a manufacturing site. Men worked five or six to a shift and often had several hours' notice before a bombing run, but targets were sometimes added after a mission had started. In support of a typical sortie, two men in the trailer locked onto an aircraft. Next to them were the board operator and an observer who monitored aircraft groundspeeds and altitude, double-checking the board operator's figures. If any changes were needed, the observer told the board operator, who could quickly adjust the bomb-release point. The men had to work swiftly to get things drawn mechanically on a vertical plotting board that had a boom with a pen on it and was covered in paper. The pen moved as the aircraft did, drawing a line to show the plane's path on a chart. The men plotted lines by hand to note where the aircraft would hit a predetermined point. They were supervised by a radar controller in radio contact with an aircrew as they reached an initial approach point that was noted at the corner of the plotting board. The time of first contact to bomb-release point was usually about 5 minutes. After the completed mission, the men tore off the sheet of plotting paper to save as backup data.

"We ran it 24-7," said John Daniel. "We normally didn't have missions all 24 hours, but we were subject to all 24."

The controller was the ranking man on the operation. Stan Sliz, a captain until he resigned his commission to join the team, handled that job on Etchberger and Daniel's crew. On the other it was done by Maj. Don Lehman. Service rank played no official part on the hill. The men called each other by their first names, far from military custom, but it was understood that the former officers were still the supervisors of the ex-enlisted men, who included computer, teletype, cryptographic, generator, radio and TACAN specialists in addition to radar technicians.

Living quarters were in an adjacent trailer where the men slept in bunks. Someone normally rested in a sleeping bag on the floor of the work center. Cable stretched between the trailers so the man on watch could notify the others when a new frag was received. Daniel remembers having that duty and calling the sleeping quarters to alert men to report. The operation went smoothly from the beginning and the project's impact was immediately noticeable—to the United States and to the enemy, Clayton said. Bomb damage assessments were done after each mission; the men reviewed them upon their return to Udorn. These showed that bombing results had improved dramatically very quickly. If the North Vietnamese tied the increased Phou Pha Thi activity to the more accurate bombing of Hanoi, it was a given that they would try to knock out the equipment.

"When this came along, all of a sudden terror started coming out of the skies and we knew it wasn't going to take them very long to figure out what the hell was going on," said Clayton. "(The Hanoi area) was bombed during bad weather day after day after day. We knew that they were going to come after us, eventually, which is what happened. They couldn't afford to let that continue."

8

As the Project Heavy Green men launched their mission with his tepid blessing, Lao premier Prince Souvanna Phouma left his homeland for a month-long trip including visits to New York City, Washington and Paris. He met with President Johnson twice at the White House. On Friday, October 20, 1967, they posed together for photos on the South Lawn before having lunch with Secretary of State Dean Rusk, Secretary of Defense Robert McNamara, several Lao officials and others. The two leaders met again the next day with Vice President Hubert Humphrey, Rusk, McNamara, presidential adviser Marvin Watson, a Lao contingent and various other U.S. representatives. As they talked this second time, the first national protest against the Vietnam War was happening nearby on the National Mall. The 50,000-strong gathering culminated with a march on the Pentagon that dissolved into violence and ended with nearly 700 arrests.

Johnson spoke plainly with his advisers—whom he had recently stunned by saying he was considering not running for re-election—and in a series of October conversations with members of the news media.

"I am unhappy that we have not found an answer in Vietnam. I hope we can," Johnson said during an off-the-record October meeting with 16 news editors from foreign nations. The president told the newsmen that Ellsworth Bunker, U.S. ambassador to South Vietnam, predicted that history would record Vietnam as another Korea if America had "the patience and will to stay the course." Johnson informed the editors that the people of South Vietnam had been bombed daily a month earlier in the lead-up to the country's vote for president.

"It's been said that (the communists) killed more civilians in four weeks trying to keep them from voting before the election than our

American bombers killed in the big cities of North Vietnam in bombing military targets," he said. "We are seeking maximum deterrent with minimum loss of life. We try to minimize civilian losses. If we were to stop the bombing, the cost in lives would be a great deal more. There are a half-million North Vietnamese tied down repairing the damage caused by the bombing."

Johnson told the editors that the United States was in Southeast Asia because of its commitment to its allies and to permit the South Vietnamese the right of self-determination. He said he wanted peace "stronger than anybody in the world except perhaps for those Marines on the (Vietnamese Demilitarized Zone) tonight." He said he could be a "temporary hero" like British Prime Minster Neville Chamberlain, who returned from a September 1938 meeting in Munich with the Nazis' assurance that they would stop their outward advancement after annexing the Sudetenland.

"We could easily spend our money on bread and butter and schools rather than on bombs and guns, but we believe our present policy is the best one, and we will do everything we can to try to bring peace as soon as possible," Johnson said.

Earlier in October, Johnson met in his office with *Washington Post* reporter Chalmers Roberts, who told the president he was convinced that the discontent in the United States must be a factor in the thinking of Hanoi and Beijing. The president agreed before speaking about the war positions of Republicans and Democrats.

"If you look at the past, you will find that politicians will be against the things which are unpopular and for the things which are popular," said Johnson. "There is more dissent on the Vietnam issue than we would like. It makes those that fight the war do even more."

Secretary Rusk put the war in a bigger frame earlier that week, Roberts said, by looking at the whole of Asia and problems with China.

"(Australian) Prime Minister (Robert) Menzies told me that we need to make more statements about how we got into Vietnam, why we are there and our reasons for staying," said Johnson. "He said that we need to repeat these speeches. I got the best response to my San Antonio speech (a week or so earlier) than to any I have given."

Roberts asked Johnson if he had heard anything recently from Hanoi.

"I couldn't tell you anything if I did have it," he said. "We are in touch with them, much more direct and authoritative than you could know. But from all I have seen, they have not budged one bit. They still want four things: recognize the National Front of Liberation (the Vietcong); stop the bombing; retreat; and get out of Vietnam. I wish my people were as solid in support of my soldiers as Ho's people are solid in support for his troops. This is not Johnson's war. This is America's war. If I drop dead tomorrow, this war will still be with you."

On October 23, the president met with Joe Lastelic of the *Kansas City Star*, which was planning a series on the upcoming presidential campaigns. Johnson said the war would, of course, be an issue in the race.

"But all of us, regardless of party, want peace. The question is how we get it. The prudent, careful man will not seek a wider war or a surrender," he said.

Upon Souvanna Phouma's return from abroad October 26, he met for an hour in Vientiane with Ambassador Sullivan before leaving on another trip. In a cable he sent to Secretary Rusk, Sullivan said the men didn't talk about "more sensitive matters" due to the presence of a Lao cabinet member and said he was "unable to make any deep soundings into his mood."

"(Souvanna) seemed vigorous and bouncy and showed no external signs of depression. In passing small talk, he remarked with considerable pleasure on the treatment he received in Washington, especially at the White House."

Sullivan's cable said there was general satisfaction among the Lao regarding the manner in which the prime minister had been received in the United States. The fact that President Johnson had granted him a second lunch meeting was interpreted as a mark of special recognition for Souvanna, the ambassador said.

After the North Vietnamese rejected America's latest attempt at negotiations made during Johnson's San Antonio speech, the United States moved forward with its bombing campaign aided by the new radar system in place on Phou Pha Thi.

9

The men on each half of the Heavy Green team were about equal in their level of experience. Though Dick Etchberger was two ranks higher than his counterpart on the other squad, that group had a fine senior NCO in Master Sgt. James H. Calfee, 35, a native of Newgulf, Texas.

"He was a heck of a nice guy," said John Daniel, a board operator who knew him from previous temporary duty work. "He was a good radar guy, a good senior NCO."

Daniel, who worked on the squad led by Stan Sliz and Etchberger, also thought highly of co-worker Staff Sgt. Bill Husband, a power production specialist.

"He did his job and whatnot as good as anybody," he said.

Before each 12-hour shift, the men did pre-operational checks to make sure "equipment was in tolerance, that everything was right, you know, so we could have a degree of accuracy," said Daniel. "We'd run checks to make sure so we could adjust it and have everything ready to go. There were a lot of snags, problems that we had to solve. Not everything ran smoothly. There were things that happened that weren't anything that we had anticipated."

Though the men weren't expecting to experience combat, there were no guarantees. Six airmen from the 1st Combat Evaluation Group, their same parent unit in Louisiana, had been killed in an ambush the previous year while surveying a planned radar site in Dong Ha, South Vietnam.

Heavy Green work was largely the same one day to the next. The target locations were sent via secure messaging to the men who input the data into a computer portion of the system and charted the paths the aircrews would follow. To maintain security, all of the transmissions went out scrambled on a dedicated mission frequency. The main communicator with the bomb crew was the controller. When he pressed a button on his radio microphone, the words he spoke went out as a "whoosh" to an Airborne Warning and Control System aircraft flying a pattern above the Gulf of Tonkin. The airplane's equipment decoded and retransmitted it a moment later on a separate attack frequency so the bombing run aircrews could receive the information. Sliz said AWACS aircrews kept their plane flying straight and level during transmission because turning it could interfere with the signal and the men on the bombing run wouldn't get a clear message from the peak. Project Heavy Green was part of a larger Air Force undertaking called Combat Skyspot in which men placed radar systems throughout Southeast Asia to direct friendly aircrews to targets. Before that mission started in 1965, bomb targeting in Southeast Asia was rather unsophisticated.

"A Strategic Air Command liaison officer with a transponder beacon would sit in a helicopter or on a ridge over a known point so a bomb aircrew could come in and aim at the signal and offset coordinates from it," Sliz said. "(Aircraft equipment) was weather avoidance and air-intercept radar. You could pick up another aircraft, that's it. In the jungle, radar worked poorly because there was nothing for it to bounce off of, really."

Heavy Green men on the mountain quickly saw that the enemy was building a road toward their location. There was really no way to disguise all of the preparation done atop the mountain since it involved explosives and multiple helicopter flights, so the enemy likely knew the Americans were up to something since before Clayton's team ever started its work. The CIA employed Lao and Hmong tribesman to track enemy movements in the valley beneath Phou Pha Thi. The Heavy Green controllers, Sliz and Don Lehman, were in constant contact with the peak's CIA staff and Thai mercenaries to plan aerial attacks on the roadwork. American aircrews damaged it, which delayed—but never truly halted—its construction. These bombing runs sometimes brought aircraft directly over the mountain, filling the Americans with pride at the sight and sound. If any of the men was nervous about the work location, he didn't show it to his comrades. Each was certain of his skills, as was their commander, Jerry Clayton, whose confidence in his radar men was high. It was less so with the tactical air navigation system mission that had been thrust upon him at the last minute. Running that equipment consumed much of his time due to their unfamiliarity with it.

"(It) turned out that we had an odd TACAN to run that only one of the men assigned had ever seen," Clayton said. "On the other hand, the people that were operating (the radar equipment) were handpicked by me personally. The least of my worries was (the radar team). They knew what they were doing."

If the Project Heavy Green men got a direct flight from Udorn, the trip to the mountain was only about two hours by helicopter. Often though, they had to make stops along the way and were left unarmed at one Lima site where they waited for another chopper to arrive to continue their journey.

"They would drop us, and we'd be there all by ourselves except a (CIA) guy in his hut, and we'd just sit there and wait 'til another chopper came to take us to the next spot," said Sliz.

At one such stop, he recalls unarmed white men in military uniforms walking right past them. He took them for Russians. Neither party said a word to the other.

"They were doing their thing. We were doing ours," he said. "They were Caucasians and they weren't Americans. They were doing their own covert stuff."

Clayton, the Heavy Green commander, made several trips to the mountain that fall, staying for a couple of days on the first visit. He never spent another night on the peak for concern of getting trapped there due to the weather as he was needed at the operation's Udorn headquarters.

"Once you got stuck in one of those places, you never knew when you would get out," he said, noting that nobody at Udorn questioned him about his unit's mission or the movements of his men. "There was so much going on over there (that was) spooky that people kind of, you know, (simply said) 'Here's another one.' We actually out-spooked ourselves."

Though the setting was austere and the men knew the enemy surrounded them, life on the mountain wasn't too tough, Daniel and

Sliz recalled. The work was tedious and mentally demanding, but not strenuous. The men had time to play cards or write letters to loved ones after completing their shifts and extra camp duties.

"Hopefully the weather held out so you could get a chopper in to get mail out and mail in," said Daniel. "We never knew what the weather was going to do, how it was going to cooperate."

The men slept on bunks in a trailer and quickly obtained some materials at Udorn to construct an addition with a day room, dining room, lounge area and with an electric range and refrigerators that ran on diesel generators. They had a plywood latrine with toilet seats. Waste was simply collected in 55-gallon metal drums and burned by adding diesel fuel. When they weren't working, they tried to make the peak more comfortable for themselves. They procured their own food at Udorn for when they headed back. They got steaks, chicken, pork chops and coffee from an Army mess sergeant in exchange for some building materials.

"We ate good," said Daniel, who remembers doing some plumbing work at a Udorn snack bar in exchange for supplies.

They brought some beer with them once and had a ration of one or two a day. The men on rest and relaxation time at Udorn made sure that those on the hill got replacement supplies when needed. One of the off-duty GIs rode in the chopper to ensure the transfer of goods happened as things just sometimes disappeared in Southeast Asia if nobody was watching. Even a ramrod-straight career GI like Etchberger was known to get in on the act, according to his commander, who admiringly described him as a "master scrounger."

"Dick was a jewel in our little venture in Laos, where strong leadership and technical knowledge were musts for everyone. He just about carried his crew," said Clayton. "He procured parts from a supply system there at Udorn that was in its infancy with the stock piled out on (the aircraft flightline) in no particular order."

Etch wasn't averse to breaking through military bureaucracy when he felt it made no sense, either. His comrades remember him playing a crucial decoy role in the theft of a truck. Some CIA men in the field needed a reliable vehicle but received no help in getting one from the motor pool staff at Udorn. Instead of banging his head against the wall in frustration, Etch simply distracted a clerk with conversation while some co-conspirators loaded a vehicle onto a waiting aircraft for delivery to where it was required. Once the aircraft was airborne, Etchberger wrapped up his conversation and left the clerk to return to his work none the wiser.

Off-duty Heavy Green men in Thailand had time to golf and sightsee. One of their main destinations was Bangkok where they visited markets, had tailored suits made and toured historic temples. Clayton or his deputy, Bill Blanton, regularly visited a Bangkok bank on overnight trips to withdraw money from a special account to pay for living expenses as the bulk of the team's salaries went to United States accounts to support their families. Frank Roura, the administrative master sergeant, subbed for his bosses once and recalls bringing a briefcase containing a loaded firearm to the bank and leaving with it full of cash. Looking back on that time, he wondered what good a pistol inside of a case would have done had someone decided to rob him.

"That was an exercise," Roura remembered. "Guys dressed up in civilian clothes going to a bank in Bangkok and loading up with thousands of dollars. We were trusted with all of this kind of money. I'd sit there right in the middle of that bank and count the payroll."

While Etchberger and the others quickly adopted a work routine in Southeast Asia, their families settled into their own schedules. They were used to their husbands and fathers being away for weeks or months straight, but this time it was different because Southeast Asian tours generally lasted a year.

Kay Etchberger and her two younger sons took quickly to life in Hamburg, Dick's hometown in the Pennsylvania countryside. Rich and Cory entered fourth and third grades, respectively, in a building that served as Hamburg High School when their father was a student there. Kay was thankful to be close to her in-laws, including Dick's brother, Robert, and his wife, Martha. Dick's childhood friend Don Yocom took the boys fishing at the same places he and their father had gone as teenagers.

"Dad's family and friends immediately started keeping us busy," Rich remembers. "They would show up with a station wagon full of gear, coolers, food, fishing rods, worms. They would talk about their own families and made us feel like part of their lives. Dad's vision of having that network of friends and family there was already working out for him."

Soon after their arrival, the boys participated in a Hamburg tradition of using water-based paints to create Halloween scenes on the windows of downtown shops. Cory remembers his mother taking a photo of him with a rendering of a witch's head he created at the five-and-dime store run by his grandfather, then sending the picture to his father overseas. Rich, older than Cory by 14 months, began working after school for his grandfather at the shop. He earned $1 a week for stocking shelves, sweeping the floor, flattening empty boxes and other simple tasks. When nobody looked, he helped himself to pieces of hand-dipped chocolate from the expensive section of the candy shelves.

"It was fun," said Rich. "A lot of the people who worked at the five-and-dime were friends of the family."

Not all Heavy Green families moved because of the mission. John Daniel's wife, Josephine, and children remained in La Junta, Colorado, and Stan Sliz's wife and children stayed put in Bismarck, North Dakota, where they had lived for nearly all of the 1960s. Frank Roura's family went to Scappoose, Oregon, his wife's hometown, while he was in Thailand. Though he only flew to the mountain once or twice, Roura was an integral part of Project Heavy Green as the commander's right-hand man and he admired his comrades' dedication to the radar mission.

"We were just part of this group—you couldn't take us apart. We were brothers, so to speak, the way we treated one another," Roura said. "They have your life in their hands, and they'd better damn well treat you that way."

After the first month or two of duty, Sliz and Lehman, the controllers of the Heavy Green crews, started to report to Tan Son Nhut Air Base in Saigon upon leaving the peak in case senior Air Force officers in charge of the air war had any questions for them.

"If nothing else, it was an excuse to get into Saigon to see a couple of friends," Sliz said. "You'd walk into the officer's club and bump into someone you'd know. You'd stay there for a day or two, then catch a ride to Bangkok for some R & R."

The controllers carried unlimited travel orders and could jump on an aircraft at any point. Sometimes Sliz would tag along with surveyors testing the equipment at each TACAN location even though it wasn't his responsibility.

"It was just something to do," he said.

Eventually, the working rhythm got so tedious that some of the men broke a camp rule about leaving the peak for no other reason than to pass the time.

10

E d Perrigo wasn't surprised that his former supervisor had been chosen for an important mission in Southeast Asia.

"He was the finest noncommissioned officer I have ever known," Perrigo recalled in a 2008 letter to Etchberger's youngest son, Cory. "Everyone liked and respected him. Unlike so many NCOs who accomplished the job through intimidation, he was soft-spoken and was a natural leader. All of us were happy to accomplish any task he assigned. (He) and I became really good friends, almost brothers."

In the same letter, Perrigo recalled meeting Cory and his brother, Rich, in the Philippines 30-plus years earlier and shared personal details with Cory about his father as a young man, including that Etch chewed gum constantly, possibly related to the cigarette habit he had quit five years earlier. Perrigo also noted that his mother-in-law thought Dick was handsome.

"Nice looks aside, he looked good in a uniform . . . like a military man," he said. "Etch was a small man in stature, but you didn't look at him as a small man."

Soon after Dick's time at Clark Air Base ended in June 1967, Perrigo reported to an assignment in Michigan before completing his own 12-month tour in Southeast Asia. Though Perrigo was not a member of Project Heavy Green, he had done plenty of sensitive work related to the war while he was with Etchberger in the Philippines. Like his mentor, he was later promoted to chief master sergeant, the service's highest enlisted rank, but retired sooner than required to retain it.

"Some of my success I owe to Etch. Since I often worked directly for him, he had the task of writing my performance reports," Perrigo wrote to Cory, who never served in the armed forces. "Promotion in the military depends on numerous factors, but perhaps the most important is a highly satisfactory performance report."

Perrigo and Etch exchanged letters in late 1967. Ed had written to Etch, and the note took some time to catch up to him because it went first to Illinois, where he had been assigned briefly prior to joining Project Heavy Green, and was forwarded to Pennsylvania before Etchberger's wife sent it to him overseas.

"It's a very long, complicated story," Etchberger replied to his friend about his presence in Thailand without mentioning his repeated forays into Laos. "I wasn't shafted. I volunteered. Fortunately, Kay understands me and she was for it, and that sure helps."

Etchberger mentioned going to Chanute Air Force Base near Rantoul, Illinois, after leaving the Philippines to work for the 2865th Ground Electronic Engineering Installation Agency. He said that he hated that job more than any duty he'd ever had in the military.

"Fortunately, too, the gods chose to smile on me and I was picked for a special project . . . to do some radar work. I volunteered for the job and here I am," he wrote. "It is the most challenging job I'll ever have in my life. I love it—travel all the time, hate to be away from home—but believe in the job and, as I said, just love it."

Etchberger closed the letter by asking Perrigo if he could get him anything in Thailand. His friend said he could and asked him to make some transfers of historic carvings on a temple by placing rice paper on them and rubbing with charcoal.

"It was sort of a thing for the tourists, and they would take them back and frame them," said Perrigo, who purchased a set for his mother-in-law previously in Bangkok but failed to get one for himself and his wife. Etch quickly complied, sending the copies in a tube originally designed to house a mortar round to Kay in Pennsylvania and asked her to forward it to his friend.

The fact that Etchberger had even considered taking a mission like Project Heavy Green at this point in his career was remarkable as he and Kay had already started making plans for their lives after the military.

"When I leave here I may be on my last assignment," he wrote to Perrigo. "Haven't made my decision yet. Although the wife and I are talking about a (subsequent) tour to Europe."

Military service often comes with being separated from loved ones for extended periods, but by the nature of radar bomb scoring work, each of the Heavy Green men had been away from his family more than the average GI. Still, late 1967 was the first time Etchberger had spent the holidays apart from his wife and young sons. Dick's family wasn't particularly religious in his youth, only attending services on Easter Sunday and Christmas at the United Church of Christ. In Hamburg, Kay prepared to celebrate the holidays with her in-laws and her two younger sons. Having a grandfather who managed a store with a basement display of toys for sale was a great benefit at this time of year, Cory Etchberger remembers.

"We always had the neatest, newest toys, especially military ones," he said. "I mean, to have a grandfather who had access to such cool toys was a young boy's dream."

Red Etchberger converted a corner of the store basement into an area where children could sit on Santa's lap and tell him what they would like for Christmas.

"It was too cool. Our grandpa knew Santa," said Cory, who recalls his grandparents doting on him and Rich that Christmas, possibly more than they would have if their father wasn't overseas with the military. Rich recalls the minister from the family's church purchasing candy from Miller's 5 & 10 to distribute during Christmas services and now suspects that his grandfather's semiannual church visits had as much to do with his wallet as his faith.

"I think it was more of a business visit for Grandpa than anything," he said.

Cory's most vivid memory of this time is giving a girl in his third grade class a present of a powder-puff meant for his schoolteacher and presenting the gift meant for the student to the educator after wrapping them himself and mislabeling them. As presents from their parents, the boys each received rings and silver bracelets with their names engraved on them. Rich remembers not being able to wear the bracelet for years because it was too loose on his thin wrist. Cory recalls thinking it strange to receive a gift mentioning his father since he was gone at the time.

Dick Etchberger spent Christmas 1967 working on Phou Pha Thi. His teammates Stan Sliz and John Daniel don't recall anything out of the ordinary happening at their location that day. It was just another typical workday for them. Stan remembers hearing a U.S. pilot saying "Merry Christmas, zipperheads" while dropping bombs on a road construction site after being guided to the target by the Project Heavy Green staff.

Commander Jerry Clayton had his hands full that day at Udorn Air Base. Before sunrise Dec. 25, enemy soldiers attacked Lima Site 61 in Muang Phalane, Laos, where some of Clayton's other men ran a TACAN system. Rockets and mortars hit it and the sleeping quarters of Staff Sgt. John D. Morris, 25, and Sgt. Peter W. Scott, 22, killing both. Men on an Air America chopper made it to the site long enough to confirm the airmen were dead, then retreated under heavy fire. It was five more days before they could recover the bodies.

"The Lao or the Thais declined to furnish any reliable security force for the nav aids people," said Clayton. "The Lao ran every time there was a scare and, as a result, the two men manning the site were killed in their sleep. The guards were nowhere to be found."

11

n early 1968, the enemy-built road continued to creep toward Phou Pha Thi, and no Project Heavy Green man believed Lima Site 85 would escape an attack. Radar controller Stan Sliz recalls looking at North Vietnamese soldiers through powerful binoculars and trading obscene gestures with them just for laughs despite the seriousness of the matter.

"We threw fingers at each other," he recalled.

The main question the Americans had was, "When would an assault occur?" How an offensive would happen seemed predictable enough to the men: the North Vietnamese Army was carving a road through the jungle so it could get big guns close enough to use in an attempt to soften up the defenses on the mountain's flanks. Ground forces would then mount an attack and try to reach the 5,800-foot peak. An aerial assault by the enemy never crossed anyone's mind as a possibility, but that's precisely what happened in the early afternoon of January 12, 1968, when the NVA launched a peculiar mission that may have been the only air attack on U.S. forces in the war.

Just after lunchtime that day, board operator John Daniel hiked down to the landing pad near the CIA trailer to meet an Air America resupply chopper flown by pilot Theodore H. Moore and flight mechanic Glenn R. Woods. Moore was a former Army pilot who had flown for Air America for just six months, but he had extensive experience flying in South Vietnam. As Daniel finished unloading the helicopter, an unusual noise drew his attention skyward.

"I looked up and (thought) 'Gosh, oh mighty, what it this?' There was a couple of biplanes going over," he said. "(I) didn't know what the hell it was."

It was an unsophisticated attack by two dark-green, single-engine Antonov AN-2 Colts built in the Soviet Union and flown 160 miles by North Vietnamese Army pilots from a base near Hanoi. These weren't crop dusters. Colts are the largest single-engine biplanes ever produced and have room inside for additional crewmembers. By 1968, they had been in production for 20 years and were valued for their adaptability to various missions. They were capable of slow flight and able to use unimproved runways. These Colts had been modified for fighting. They had Russian-made 57-mm rockets in pods under their wings, and their floors were adapted with metal tubes so soldiers behind the pilot could drop 120-mm mortars toward targets below. The aircraft had flown in a formation with two other Colts, whose pilots observed the actions of their countrymen from a few miles away.

Lima Site 85 had no antiaircraft defense other than small arms carried by Thai and Lao guards. The only weapon an American radar man may have possessed was a personal sidearm carried by Tech Sgt. Donald "Monk" Springsteadah, a radar technician, without the knowledge of his superiors. Stan Sliz was with an armed Thai captain at the radar camp above and away from the helipad when the biplane attack started. He couldn't believe his eyes.

"It was like seeing something out of the Spanish Revolution," he said.

As the two primary airplanes approached the peak, the Thai officer next to him raised his rifle and fired just before the pilot of the closest aircraft shot rockets toward them. When hit, the plane jerked upward, causing the rockets to pass over their heads, Sliz said. Daniel saw the action from the helipad below.

"They salvoed a bunch of rockets," he said. "We could see 'em. We seen the rounds go off and, goddamn, they missed the radar equipment. It was a hell of a deal. You just wouldn't believe a biplane attack happening in almost 1970."

As the pilots fired rockets, other biplane crewmen dropped mortars through the fabricated floor tubes of the AN-2s. The explosives became armed in the slipstream and detonated on impact. The strategy was largely ineffective because it did no damage to the immobile Air America helicopter that was in plain sight or the radar equipment swathed in camouflage netting. Moore and Woods decided to give chase and dashed to their blue and white chopper. Moore started it, and they were soon in the air. Woods reached for an AK-47 rifle, hoping to use the Soviet firearm to fire upon a Russian-built aircraft. Moore had 1,000-plus hours in Hueys, which had a top speed of 135 mph. The Colts, however, were powered by 1,000-horsepower, 9-cylinder engines and could reach 160 mph.

The Air America duo sped after the biplanes, one of which seemed to be struggling. Witnesses cited in a later Air Force report estimated that the plane was flying at about 120 mph, meaning a modern helicopter with a skilled pilot at the controls could successfully give chase to it, which is exactly what happened. Moore and Woods trailed the lagging Colt, possibly the one hit by the Thai officer's gunfire, before overtaking it from above. Woods leaned out of an open door and unleashed a burst of gunfire into the enemy cockpit. He watched in amazement as it began to lose altitude and crashed into a hillside. The Americans then chased down the second Colt. Moore piloted his chopper close to this biplane and Woods again opened fire, hitting it multiple times. The second plane crashed about three miles from the first, while the North Vietnamese crews observing from the remaining Colts escaped back to their homeland.

According to an Air Force Contemporary Historical Examination of Current Operations (CHECO) project report on Lima Site 85 compiled that summer, the North Vietnamese attack on the peak killed four Hmong, but the radar system suffered no damage, and the team's work continued without interruption. Daniel and Sliz clearly recalled their team supporting bombing runs the night of the biplane assault.

Within a few days, an American Chinook helicopter crew retrieved the wreckage of one Colt and brought it to Lima Site 85. There, the Heavy Green men saw for themselves that tubes had been welded to openings in the floor to allow mortars to pass through them. The biplane was later displayed in the capital of Vientiane as proof of North Vietnam's presence in Laos while nothing was said about the U.S. mission as being the target. The American Embassy sent a cable to Washington, D.C., mentioning the attack on the Phou Pha Thi "navigation facility" but made no reference to the radar equipment there.

"We can conclude that aerial attack represented enemy effort to get at (the) navigation facility which could be reached on ground only at heavy cost," the cable said. "Theoretically, enemy could resort to this technique again, either at Site 85 or elsewhere. However, it should be noted that this attack was largely unsuccessful and two (enemy) aircraft were lost. On basis of available information we regard aerial raid as highly unusual variation in normal pattern of enemy tactics and do not believe this one incident necessarily introduces new dimension to war in Laos . . . we are presently reviewing questions of air defense at Site 85 . . ."

The CHECO report mentions that three captured antiaircraft guns soon reinforced air defense of the peak, but in 2012 interviews neither Stan Sliz nor John Daniel recalled any large weapons being brought to the mountain. The team soon received 10 M-16s, a case of ammunition and survival vests containing tiny radios, flares and other emergency items. Sliz said a team of Thai guards held a training session to familiarize the radar men with the firearms. Etchberger and Master Sgt. James H. Calfee, senior sergeant on the second team, conducted some training in them, too, team member Staff Sgt. William Husband said in a third-party interview many years after the mission. Though the enemy never attempted another air assault, a change in Heavy Green operations was underway as targets programmed by the Americans were increasingly for their own defense. By the second half of January, there were as many missions trying to halt the enemy's progress toward the mountain as were directed at targets in North Vietnam, the team's primary reason for being in Laos. More than 160 missions that month were flown within 20 miles of the peak, "mostly to the east where the threat was building," the report claims.

The CHECO account also mentions that enemy forces started pushing forward toward the base of the mountain almost immediately after the biplane attack. On January 14, 300 enemy troops were noted less than 10 miles from the mountain. Three days later, 100 were seen eight miles away "and enough concern was generated by these moves to induce Lao refugees to begin fleeing" the area around nearby Lima Site 111. While the Heavy Green men had shaken their heads at the unsophisticated and brazen manner of the biplane attack, the assault confirmed the enemy was willing to go to extraordinary and unusual lengths to disrupt their mission.

On January 17, President Johnson delivered his State of the Union address, proclaiming America's successes in Southeast Asia immediately following his opening remarks. He noted that three elections had been held in South Vietnam in the previous year "in the midst of war and under the constant threat of violence," and citizens had chosen a president, vice president, a house, a senate and local officials.

"The enemy has been defeated in battle after battle . . . (but) continues to pour men and material across frontiers and into battle, despite his continuous heavy losses," said Johnson. "He continues to hope that America's will to persevere can be broken. Well, he is wrong. America will persevere. Our patience and our perseverance will match our power. Aggression will never prevail."

Johnson said the number of South Vietnamese living in areas protected by the government had grown by more than a million since his last address, adding he was prepared for peace based on the formula he proposed during his San Antonio speech four months earlier. Even as the president spoke though, the enemy was planning a massive coordinated attack that surprised America, South Vietnam and their allies two weeks later.

A January 20 CIA message predicted that "if the enemy could move in large numbers of troops into an area north of Phou Pha Thi, he would have the second jaw for a pincer movement." The first indication of a serious enemy intent to take Phou Pha Thi, the cable said, would probably be the capture of the village of Phou Den Din 7½ miles from the Project Heavy Green mountain. Phou Den Din and two other positions fell to the enemy within two days of that message. The U.S. aerial response was immediate, with more than 100 bombing missions being launched to the area in the next week.

"A pattern of encirclement of Phou Pha Thi from the north clockwise to the south was beginning to take shape," the CHECO report noted. "This pattern was not ignored by friendly forces at Phou Pha Thi. They fully realized that the enemy could mount a heavy assault against Site 85 if it was willing to accept the losses."

The enemy creeped closer through the jungle without much respite from the American barrage. On January 30 alone, 45 U.S. missions struck within 20 miles of Lima Site 85. That night, the enemy exploded mines to the south of the mountain and conducted a 30-minute mortar barrage.

"The (radar) commander quickly reported that, while there had been an attack near the site, it amounted to no more than a probe," the CHECO report reads. "Later assessments confirmed that no enemy troops had reached the top of the ridge; only the bottom defenses had been tested."

America's mettle was shaken elsewhere in a dramatic way when tens of thousands of North Vietnamese and Vietcong forces launched the Tet Offensive overnight January 30-31. The simultaneous attacks startled American and South Vietnamese forces and required a massive response over the next month.

12

The Tet Offensive had little or no effect on Project Heavy Green because its targets were far from Phou Pha Thi in Laos and Udorn Air Base in Thailand, the mission's two work locations. So named because it began on the Vietnamese lunar New Year of Tet, the surprise and breadth of the coordinated series of attacks shocked South Vietnam, the U.S. and its allies. Stan Sliz, the radar controller on the crew that also included Dick Etchberger, was aboard a T-39 Sabreliner executive jet bound for Tan Son Nhut Air Base in Saigon when the attacks began.

After being on the peak for two weeks, Sliz enjoyed the freedom such journeys afforded. The Illinois native may have had the most time in Southeast Asia of anyone on Project Heavy Green. He first visited Thailand and Vietnam in the mid-1950s while serving as an aide to a general at Pacific Air Forces headquarters in Hawaii. He flew into Saigon shortly after the French defeat there and spoke about it wistfully during an October 2012 interview at his home in Huntington Beach, California.

"That's when Saigon was really, truly, the Paris of the Orient: wide boulevards, sidewalk cafes and rooftop restaurants. We were welcomed by a French Foreign Legion ceremony full of pomp and circumstance. It was much different a decade later: drudgery and garbage since the war. It wasn't the same Saigon."

When the city fell under attack during Tet, he and the T-39 aircrew were held in Bangkok for a few hours before being allowed to proceed. Saigon was desolate with trails of smoke and no activity visible from the air other than helicopters flying back and forth. The pilot of his plane made a steep approach to the Tan Son Nhut runway because of attack concerns. Sliz spent that night in a bunker on the base with friends, chatting about what might happen next. In his case, it turned out not to be much; he left the next day and made his way back to Thailand.

"They decided I didn't have to stick around, and I jumped on the first aircraft out of there. So I didn't see much of Tet other than the remnants and being a part of all of the paranoia that was going on."

Most of the Project Heavy Green men traveled at least a bit in their off time, including making the 700-mile round-trip to Bangkok. Sliz's restlessness may explain why he and a handful of other Americans took an unusual—and prohibited—risk in February by hiking down the mountain to see villagers who had requested a meeting with "the blond king of the mountain," meaning him. CIA staffers set up the introduction and hiked off the hill with Sliz, Etchberger, Springsteadah and Husband.

Even if the Americans didn't have M-16s when they left the peak, friendly guards were positioned along the way, and Springsteadah had smuggled a personal sidearm to Southeast Asia and may have had it on him for protection. In an interview many years after the mission, Husband said "a lot" of the men had visited the village previously.

There was assumed risk simply by heading toward the valley where enemy forces were scattered. Construction of a road toward the mountain had been noticeable for weeks, if not months. The men could see it being built and directed aircraft to drop ordnance on it in a lingering game of cat and mouse. American aircrews bombed it during the day. The enemy would make repairs to it at night, after which the United States would hit the route again. Sliz may have been emboldened to leave the peak as he was in constant contact with the CIA men, who stayed abreast of the road's progress and enemy movements in general by sending small teams of Lao and Hmong forces into the jungle.

Still, they made the hike toward danger, knowing that the enemy was slowly making progress in building a road toward the mountain. Within 12 weeks of the mission's launch, Project Heavy Green was focusing on more targets in Laos than in North Vietnam. Half of the missions they supported in February were in their own area, and that percentage would only grow in the coming weeks. So why chance a confrontation by visiting the village? Were the men lulled into a false sense of security by the skill they had in their work and the overwhelming firepower they could summon? It may have been nothing more than boredom that led them to take such a risk, but leaving the hill while enemy forces were in the valley beneath was impetuous, if not reckless, and their commander, Jerry Clayton, was furious when he learned about it later.

Whatever pushed them to leave their camp, even if it was just curiosity, the men knew they were breaking a steadfast rule to remain on the peak. Sliz and Etchberger, in particular, were essential senior members of their squad and their teammates would not have had the knowledge, let alone the authority, to fill their roles had harm come to them. Despite any danger, the trip turned out to be uneventful and the men safely returned to the peak. While in the valley, they participated in a native ceremony in which a shaman put string bracelets on their wrists for good luck. Sliz had his on a week or two later when he visited the officers' club at Udorn Air Base. A Thai waitress there recognized it and urged him not to remove it. He didn't. Four decades later, he shrugged off the trip down the mountain as having been no big deal, saying he and the other men were likely just bored and trusted the villagers as some of the mountain's security forces lived with them. However, he also acknowledged that there was more cause for concern in February than there was even just a month earlier. The valley was alive with forces from both sides. In mid-February, a Hmong patrol ambushed a small North Vietnamese Army unit and killed some enemy soldiers. A notebook on one of the bodies had details of a pending attack and "TACAN" written in English with an accurate location of the tactical air navigation equipment atop Phou Pha Thi.

The Americans were given the OK to direct attacks against any validated target within 7.5 miles of the peak. If under imminent threat, they could direct strike aircraft in clear voice transactions which, if intercepted by the enemy, would be valuable in proving American presence in Laos. An Air Force forward air controller arrived to direct airstrikes against encroaching communist forces. In February, 473 strike sorties were flown within 19 miles of the mountain; of these, one-third were radar-directed. The others were close enough for the forward air controller to direct by sight. He was joined by another forward air controller who carried on alone after a few days when the original one left the peak.

"The advancing North Vietnamese forces, whose very presence should have triggered closure of the radar facility, had become a reason to maintain it," Dr. Tim Castle wrote in *One Day Too Long*, his 1999 book about Project Heavy Green's role in the North Vietnam bombing campaign. "The opportunity to kill large numbers of North Vietnamese and Pathet Lao soldiers was irresistible."

Ambassador William Sullivan directed Vientiane CIA station chief Ted Shackley to prepare a risk assessment, including a projected date as to how soon an attack on Phou Pha Thi might occur. The study concluded that date as March 10, and Sullivan sent word of that conclusion to Air Force Chief of Staff Gen. John P. McConnell in Washington.

In preparation for an assault, CIA staffers Terry Quill and Woody Spence at Site 85 collected intelligence and reviewed the mountain's protective operations. They studied the peak and set up protective positions featuring concertina wire and land mines. They installed a portable launcher for white phosphorous rockets. In late February, Quill left the peak for a break and was replaced by his supervisor, Howard Freeman, who normally worked at Lima Site 36 nearby. A chopper crew brought a 105mm howitzer to the peak with a captured enemy 85mm field gun that was set up near the helipad. The Air Force technicians attached explosives to their equipment so they could destroy it if they had to flee. Amidst all of this activity, normal movement of Project Heavy Green men continued between the peak and Udorn Air Base.

President Johnson had much of his time this month consumed by the war. He took a two-day cross-country trip to meet with troops leaving for Vietnam. On February 17, he visited Fort Bragg, North Carolina, and El Toro Marine Corps Station, California. The next day he went to San Diego to address sailors aboard the U.S.S. Constellation aircraft carrier and then to golf with former President Eisenhower in Palm Desert, California. Johnson returned to the White House to meet with United Nations Secretary General U. Thant of Burma before retreating to his Texas ranch for a few days. He came back to Washington in time to hear CBS News anchorman Walter Cronkite, fresh from a visit to Southeast Asia, end his nightly newscast in an unusual manner. The veteran broadcast journalist presented an opinion piece saying he no longer expected the United States and its allies to outright win the Vietnam War. He believed it would end in "negotiations, not the dictation of peace terms."

"To say that we are closer to victory today is to believe, in the face of the evidence, the optimists who have been wrong in the past. To suggest we are on the edge of defeat is to yield to unreasonable pessimism. To say that we are mired in stalemate seems the only realistic, yet unsatisfactory, conclusion," said Cronkite. He added that he found it increasingly clear that the "only rational way out then will be to negotiate, not as victors, but as an honorable people who lived up to their pledge to defend democracy, and did the best they could."

With the respected newsman's words fresh in his mind, Johnson attended a Pentagon ceremony the next day for Secretary of Defense Robert McNamara as he left his post after seven years on the job. In addressing McNamara's performance, the president's words were muted and awkward, calling the secretary a "textbook example of the modern public servant."

"But I suspect there are many others out there before me now in uniform and in civilian clothes, high ranking and not so high ranking, who also qualify as modern public servants," Johnson said. "I want to say to each of you that your country is grateful to you for the quality of the work that you do on behalf of all of us, as your country is grateful to this good man, Bob McNamara, to whom we have come here today to say goodbye and farewell."

He was succeeded by Washington attorney Clark Clifford, who had been involved with defense issues and politics in the nation's capital since World War II. A past member of President Kenney's Foreign Intelligence Advisory Board, Clifford took over the top defense post March 1, not long after he had visited Southeast Asia with retired Army Gen. Maxwell Taylor, former U.S. ambassador to South Vietnam and past chairman of the Joint Chiefs of Staff.

A third of the world away, Sliz and Etchberger returned to the peak Monday, March 4, with the nine men of their crew: Daniel, Springsteadah, Mel Holland, Pat Shannon, Henry Gish, Jack Starling, James Davis, Don Worley and William Husband. Clayton, the mission commander, was in contact all week with Ambassador Sullivan in Vientiane about how long to leave the men on the job there.

He hoped to bring them back safely to Thailand, but it wasn't Clayton's call. Pacific Air Forces Commander Gen. John D. Ryan also wanted to initiate a retreat from the site, but despite being a four-star general, he also didn't have the final say to end the mission. The ambassador did, and he already had a report saying the site couldn't be held past March 10. Still, no call to evacuate was made. Maj. Gen. William C. Lindley Jr., deputy commander of 7th/13th Air Force, cabled Ryan that pressure be maintained on Ambassador Sullivan to protect "the site at all costs." In fact, Air Force leaders in Saigon wanted to increase the number of Heavy Green men on the peak. Sullivan acquiesced, allowing two complete radar teams of five men to be on the mountain at the same time so it could be used 24 hours a day right up until any future evacuation. The non-radar positions—computer, teletype, cryptographic, generator, radio and TACAN specialists—would remain singly staffed.

Neither Clayton nor his deputy, Lt. Col. Bill Blanton, normally rotated with either of the crews. One of them might go up to the site to check on things but only stay for as long as it took to switch out the technicians before returning to Udorn with those men heading back to Thailand. After consulting with the ambassador, though, Clayton decided to send Blanton to the peak with four others from the team run by radar controller Don Lehman, who would remain at Udorn. Reporting to the peak Saturday, March 9, with Blanton were Master Sgt. James Calfee, Tech Sgts. Herbert A. Kirk and Willis R. Hall, and Sgt. David S. Price, a radar technician who had been serving in a logistics supply position at Udorn Air Base since arriving in Southeast Asia with the others five months earlier. It was Price's first working visit to the peak. There were now 19 Americans on the hill: 16 at the Heavy Green camp and three, including the Air Force combat controller, at the CIA's nearby position. A concerned Clayton kept tabs from Udorn, but the career GI had no qualms following the ambassador's orders.

"To me, 'hold at all costs' meant only one thing: hold at all costs and, all costs, strangely enough, when it comes to what you're doing for your country, means to lie to the people," said Clayton. "I didn't like it, but there wasn't too much I could do about it. The ambassador told me in no uncertain words that he was final authority on everything that happened up there."

Dick Etchberger, about age 9, at St. John's Lutheran Church in Hamburg, Pennsylvania.

Dick (left) with his older brother, Robert, at the back of their home in Hamburg, circa 1946.

Dick with his mother, Kathryn, and father, Donald, at their home, circa 1948.

Dick Etchberger as a high school student, circa 1950.

Etchberger during Air Force basic training in 1951 at Sampson Air Force Base near Seneca Lake, New York.

Airman 3rd Class Etchberger, circa 1952.

Airman 3rd Class Etchberger, likely in 1952 when he was a student in a basic electronics course at Keesler Air Force Base in Biloxi, Mississippi.

Airman 2nd Class Dick Etchberger (front row, far left) with classmates from a radar bomb scoring class Oct. 15, 1952, at Keesler Air Force Base, Mississippi. He completed this course after attending one in electronics fundamentals there.

While home on leave from the service, circa 1953, Dick Etchberger (far right) visits with his parents, brother Robert (far left) and Robert's fiancée, Martha Corell, who later became his wife.

Dick Etchberger in the cockpit of a T-6 Texan trainer in summer 1953 when he was in the Air Force's Aviation Cadet Training Program at Spence Air Force Base in Moultrie, Georgia. Repercussions from a head injury he suffered as a teenager ended his chance at flying for the service.

Donald and Kathryn Etchberger (left) in a Marrakesh, Morocco, restaurant with grandson Steve Wilson, daughter-in-law Kay Etchberger and their son, Dick, in 1959 when he was stationed in the northwest African country with the Air Force.

Kay and Dick Etchberger in 1959 with their infant son, Cory, in Marrakesh, Morocco.

Dick Etchberger in 1962 with sons Rich (left) and Cory in their home at Fort Lincoln in Bismarck, North Dakota.

Capt. Stan Sliz (left) and Capt. Tom Reeves with Senior Master Sgt. Dick Etchberger in 1963 at a formal function in North Dakota, where the men served in Detachment 10 of the 11th Radar Bomb Scoring Squadron. Sliz and Etchberger would work together four years later on Project Heavy Green in Laos.

Dick Etchberger as a master sergeant in 1962.

Senior Master Sgt. Dick Etchberger, possibly at Clark Air Base in the Philippines, where he was assigned from 1965–1967.

President Lyndon B. Johnson (center) meets Aug. 1, 1967, with advisers (clockwise from left) McGeorge Bundy, Secretary of State Dean Rusk, Deputy Secretary of Defense Paul Nitze, White House Press Secretary George Christian and Special Assistant for National Security Affairs Walt Rostow. North Vietnam bombing strategy was a constant topic of discussion during this period. (White House photo)

U.S. Ambassador to Laos William H. Sullivan (Courtesy National Archives, photo no. 59-SO-318-1)

Lao Prime Minister Souvanna Phouma

The American radar and tactical air navigation setup atop Phou Pha Thi, Laos. (U.S. Air Force photo)

Col. Jerry Clayton, Project Heavy Green commander.

The cliff at Phou Pha Thi, Laos, in 1994. (U.S. Air Force photo)

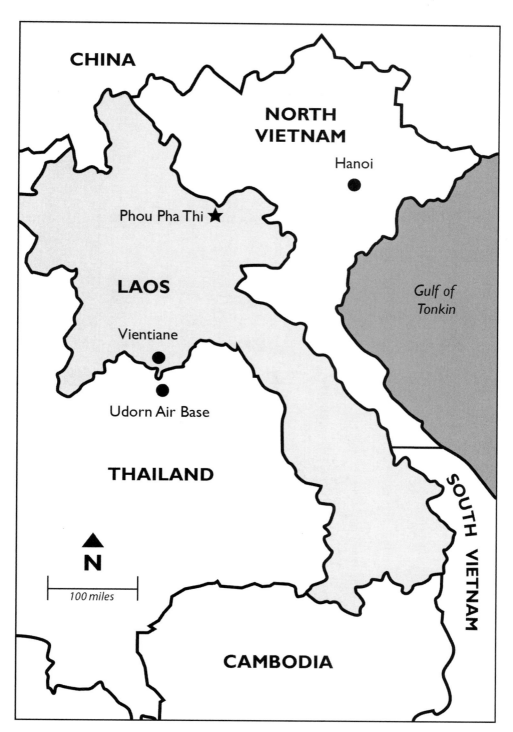

CHINA

NORTH
VIETNAM

Hanoi

Phou Pha Thi ★

LAOS

Gulf of
Tonkin

Vientiane

Udorn Air Base

THAILAND

N

100 miles

SOUTH VIETNAM

CAMBODIA

Credit: Ray Sarracino

Chief Master Sgt. Dick Etchberger at Udorn Air Base, Thailand, in late 1967 or early 1968.

President Lyndon B. Johnson (left), Secretary of Defense Robert S. McNamara, Deputy Secretary of Defense Paul Nitze and other National Security Council members discuss the Vietnam War Feb. 7, 1968. (White House photo by Yoichi Okamoto)

Project Heavy Green member John Daniel as a young sergeant (above, left) and in his La Junta, Colorado, home in April 2012.

Lima Site 85 attack survivor Stan Sliz in October 2012 (above, left) at his home in Huntington Beach, California, and as a young radar controller.

A young woman offers a flower to military police guarding the Pentagon Oct. 21, 1967, in Arlington, Virginia, during the first national protest against the Vietnam War. The same day, President Lyndon B. Johnson met at the White House with Lao Prime Minister Souvanna Phouma. (U.S. Army photo by Staff Sgt. Albert R. Simpson)

President Lyndon B. Johnson addresses the nation March 31, 1968, from the Oval Office, announcing a bombing halt in Vietnam and his intention not to seek re-election that fall. (White House photo by Yoichi Okamoto)

Air Force Chief of Staff Gen. John P. McConnell presents the Air Force Cross, the service's second-highest decoration, to Kay Etchberger in January 1969 in memory of her husband, who was killed 10 months earlier in Laos. (U.S. Air Force photo)

Air America helicopter pilot Ken Wood (above left in 1966 and right in 2010) flew three Project Heavy Green men to safety the morning of March 11, 1968. Dick Etchberger made it aboard the aircraft, too, before being shot and killed.

Rusty Irons, (above) resting on a UH-1H Huey helicopter while working for Air America and (right) in January 2011 at his home in Southern California. Irons was the crew chief who used a winch and cable to reel in four Project Heavy Green men. Note the AK-47 rifle at his arm.

Air Force Capt. Joe Panza, shown here in the 1960s, was co-pilot of the second chopper to reach Phou Pha Thi the morning of March 11, 1968. Pararescueman Staff Sgt. James J. Rogers was lowered to the peak by cable to retrieve an injured Staff Sgt. Jack Starling.

At his Half Moon Bay, California, home in November 2010, retired Air Force Chief Master Sgt. Frank Roura reads names of Project Heavy Green men he had inscribed on a commemorative mug after the fall of Lima Site 85 in March 1968. (Photo by Matt Proietti)

Don Yocom and June Kline visit the grave of classmate Dick Etchberger in August 2008. Behind them is the former high school they attended with Dick Etchberger, president of the Class of 1951. (Photo by Matt Proietti)

President Barack Obama and Dick Etchberger's sons listen as the Medal of Honor citation is read September 21, 2010. Shown are (left to right) stepson Steve Wilson, Cory Etchberger and Rich Etchberger. (U.S. Air Force photo by Jim Varhegyi)

Retired Air Force Master Sgt. Robert Dilley talks September 22, 2010, about the role he played in Dick Etchberger posthumously receiving the Medal of Honor in a White House ceremony the day prior. President Barack Obama commended Dilley for pursuing appropriate recognition for a man he'd never met. (Photo by Matt Proietti)

13

Evacuation plans for Site 85 were to be implemented only as a last resort, Maj. Gen. William C. Lindley Jr. wrote in a late-February message to three superior officers in the Pacific: his boss, 7th Air Force Commander Gen. William W. Momyer, who also was deputy chief of air operations for the Military Assistance Command, Vietnam; Gen. John D. Ryan, commander of Pacific Air Forces in Hawaii; and Lt. Gen. Benjamin O. Davis Jr., commander of 13th Air Force at Clark Air Base in the Philippines. Lindley told them that Vientiane-based CIA staff had determined the immediate threat to the mission consisted of three Pathet Lao and North Vietnamese Army battalions within the site's 12-kilometer defensive perimeter. Four other battalions were in the general area as well, while about 1,000 friendly forces were present to defend the peak.

"Our information here is that morale of the friendly forces is high and that the air strikes have demoralized the enemy so that desertions and defections even among the (North Vietnam) elements (are) increasing," said Lindley.

Citing documents recovered from a North Vietnamese officer killed February 17, Lindley explained that an enemy attack of the peak was to start from the east. A howitzer barrage and mortar attacks would precede a ground assault. Originally set for February 29, the mission was delayed due to American air strikes. The CIA estimated March 11 as the earliest date in which the enemy could resupply enough to attack. General Lindley said that 7th Air Force was in constant contact with the CIA, and a full reevaluation would be made as of that date.

Ambassador Sullivan had made several concessions to permit maximum protection of the site through air strikes. Increased attacks "should further postpone ability of enemy to attack. Combined effort along present lines should result in postponement well into . . . monsoon period when past experience indicates enemy ground actions slow almost to a halt and friendly forces traditionally take the offensive," he said in a message. General Ryan's staff at Pacific Air Forces headquarters in Hawaii had asked about the feasibility of moving the radar system, but Lindley said it was out of the question for at least six months due to non-availability of an appropriate new site and the forthcoming monsoon.

Among the enemy forces not counted in the intelligence estimates were about 20 members of the 41st Sapper Battalion of the People's Army of Vietnam. The men were assigned to the Northwest Military Region headquarters in Son La Province and led by 1st Lt. Truong Muc. They deployed to Laos in early February 1968 ahead of a planned attack on the radar operation that they planned to undertake after scaling the cliff face, which was unprotected as nobody believed it was climbable. Muc and his men would soon prove them wrong. The enemy soldiers did not use local guides and took special care to avoid contact with the valley population as Hmong guerilla commander Vang Pao's troops would have learned about any exchange between them, compromising the mission. During the planned assault, Muc would not communicate with any other units, including the artillery support that would shell Site 85 before his team attacked. The Pathet Lao would not be involved in the mission.

By Saturday, March 9, 16 Project Heavy Green men were on the peak, the most since the mission began five months earlier. Jerry Clayton's decision to not send radar controller Don Lehman on this extra rotation with other members of his crew likely saved the man's life. The same day the additional airmen arrived, a helicopter crew brought a drop fuel tank from an aircraft to the peak that the men planned to fill with napalm and rig with explosives as a defensive measure. They had already arranged to destroy the radar equipment before their eventual departure.

"And then, all of a sudden, things were really serious," said Stan Sliz.

Around sunset Sunday, March 10, John Daniel prepared to barbecue steaks for the group's dinner. The day shift on which he worked had ended at 6 p.m., and the replacement men were already at their work-stations entering the data for that night's targets. Blanton, the ranking GI on the peak, went to the CIA trailer by the helipad and was told that sources indicated the enemy was preparing to launch an attack. He called Clayton at Udorn and talked about blowing up the equipment and abandoning the camp. Blanton walked back uphill to the radar trailers and gathered his 15 men to give them the news.

"He said, 'We're in trouble,'" Daniel said. "We opted to stay over-night, have bombs dropped on (the enemy), do the night's missions as planned and hopefully get choppers in there in the morning."

Sliz agreed with Daniel's recollection.

"We had some targets already (programmed), so we decided to stick around until morning," said Sliz. "The consensus of everybody there was, 'Let's go ahead and drop bombs tonight, and we'll leave at daylight tomorrow.' Well, for us, daylight never came 'cause there was no tomorrow. Just as we made that decision, the rocket hit."

Opposing forces from the north side of the mountain fired a round into camp that exploded at the barbecue grill where some of the men had gathered near Daniel a few minutes earlier. If they hadn't gone elsewhere for Blanton's meeting, five or six men would have been killed, said Daniel.

"That was too close," said the sergeant, who believes the enemy had their coordinates. "We thought, 'We're dead. No problem. It's been a nice life, but it ain't gonna be much longer.'"

Sliz remembers noticing the nail polish remover-like smell of the rocket's cordite propellant in the air as he and the others dashed to a bunker, which was dotted with fresh shrapnel holes. No other rounds were fired, so he ran to the bunkroom to grab a survival vest and some cigarettes. Shrapnel had ruined his entire carton, leaving him with just a few in his pocket. The on-duty radar men sent a message to Udorn about the attack and checked the equipment. It was undamaged, and they returned to work intent on carrying out the night's bombing runs. Those men who weren't on duty split into groups. The CIA men invited the off-shift airmen to stay at their facility near the helipad, but they declined and opted to spend the night in sleeping bags outside the radar trailers. Etchberger and Staff Sgt. Hank Gish retrieved a radio and joined Sliz, Daniel and Springsteadah on the south side of the peak, as far as possible from where they believed the rocket had been fired. The men made contact with Clayton, their commander, at Udorn and told him of their location in the camp. Armed with a rifle, Daniel took position on a ledge under a rock overhang with Springsteadah. Aside from short bursts of small-arms fire elsewhere on the mountain, it remained relatively quiet until well after midnight. Eventually, the men slipped into sleeping bags and dozed. Unnoticed in the valley below, the North Vietnamese sappers started the 3,000-foot climb up the cliff face.

"We thought it was just as safe to stay up where we were (so) we hunkered down there," said Sliz. "(There were) typical explosions around the mountain. None of it was too close to us. Most of the stuff was happening on the perimeter. The rest of us just fell asleep on the side on the mountain. *We* weren't under direct attack. The hill was."

Blanton and Etchberger went to the CIA trailer sometime after midnight. They returned with a list of additional target coordinates to program for bombing that night and the hope that helicopter crews would extract the men at first light. At Udorn, administrative Master Sgt. Frank Roura felt helpless as he shadowed Clayton, waiting for something to do as they received updates via radio and message traffic.

"We knew that they were in duress, that the attack was imminent," said Roura. "And that's it. Then the whole thing fell apart."

At about 3:30 a.m., the hilltop came under rocket fire. Springsteadah and Daniel were protected somewhat by the rock overhang near the cliff. Sliz, Etchberger and Gish were out in the open about 25 feet away, so they crept toward the two others. Springsteadah and Daniel were on edge and were so surprised at the appearance of the men that they nearly shot their compatriots, Sliz said. The rocket barrage stopped before the NVA soldiers scaling the cliff reached the peak. Once on top, their commander, Muc, disarmed several above-ground, tripwire, antipersonnel mines and divided his men into two teams. A smaller group moved toward a Thai position about a quarter-mile from the Heavy Green trailers and took positions allowing them to fire at any forces who responded to an attack on the radar camp, their main target. Muc led the others to a spot so the trailers were between them and the cliff. A few positioned themselves where they could intercept any Americans who tried to run to the helipad and CIA location. This also allowed them to fire at anyone who came from that direction to provide aid.

A cell of NVA soldiers entered the radar operations center and opened fire, taking the on-duty Americans by surprise. Muc's men killed some of the radar men immediately, while others returned fire. His men did not try to capture any Americans, and none of them tried to surrender. Blanton was killed as he walked toward one of the enemy. A teammate reported that Tech Sgt. Herb Kirk lost his arm before being shot in the head. Thai soldiers attempted one advance toward the fighting, but withdrew after setting off a trip flare that illuminated their position. Hmong troops between the CIA helipad and the radar team's trailers advanced uphill but retreated when the North Vietnamese team fired upon them. At this point, Muc believed no Americans were successful in evading his men, but that would turn out to be false. In the alcove by the cliff, Sliz heard foreign voices above them and initially thought it could be rescuers. Etchberger saw two men coming toward them and asked aloud what he should do.

"When they get close enough, shoot 'em," Sliz said. "He shot them almost immediately as I said that. He got the two, I'm sure, but they got us. All hell broke loose."

The enemy opened fire and lobbed a series of hand grenades on the position where the five Americans were hiding. Sliz told the men to open their mouths so the concussions wouldn't shatter their teeth, something he had learned in basic officer's training. Springsteadah and Gish were quickly killed by grenades, while Sliz and Daniel suffered serious wounds to their legs.

"It was painful," said Sliz, "but once you get over the initial pain of being hit, you realize that you're still alive and talking to each other."

He drifted in and out of consciousness while Daniel remained cognizant throughout the ordeal. Etchberger was uninjured. When grenades landed near them, the men tossed the ordnance back or pushed them over the ledge with the butts of their rifles. One explosion launched Springsteadah's body off of the cliff. The men rolled Gish's body onto another grenade to absorb the blast, which knocked out Sliz or at least put him into a stupor.

"My first thought was, 'So this is what it's like to die. I wonder what the final feeling is going to be like?'" he said. "There was this bright light and (it) was almost like . . . I thought I was communicating with God, and it was like he was giving me a choice: 'Do you want to die or do you want to stay?'"

Sliz had promised his wife, Ann, that he would make it back to her. As he laid there stunned, he had a jumble of thoughts about how to do that—how to crawl down the mountain to a creek and maybe follow that to friendly villagers who could help return him to his air base in Thailand. Finally, he came to and heard Etchberger and Daniel discussing their options, including surrendering.

"I said, 'That's bullshit. Those fuckers aren't taking any prisoners,'" said Sliz. "That's when I realized I was still alive."

Etchberger and Daniel contacted a pilot overhead by radio and said they were in a shallow cave below the radar equipment. He told them alert aircraft had been launched from Nakhon Phanom Air Base, Thailand, to join the fight, along with rescue choppers from Udorn. U.S. aircraft began to attack the site just before dawn and prior to Muc's men collecting weapons, documents and equipment. The NVA soldiers took refuge from the bombs in crevices. Daniel was in touch with the pilots on a radio rescue channel.

"We called them in on ourselves. We told them to put all the ordnance they had on top of the mountain but to try to avoid the side where we were," said Daniel. "You're dead anyway. We thought, 'We might as well take some of them with us.'"

The airpower came from four A-1 Skyraiders, which operated under the call sign "Sandy" and supported search and rescue missions. Each aircraft had four 20-mm cannons and a wide assortment of bombs, rockets, grenades, flares and gun pods. They were capable of flying 325 mph but could slow down to work alongside choppers operating at less than half of that speed. They could also stay aloft for more than seven hours, making them ideal for search and rescue duty. When the Skyraiders passed overhead, the men on the cliff saw tracers following them and realized that the enemy was firing a 12.75-mm antiaircraft gun that Hmong tribesmen had given them after the biplane attack six weeks earlier.

Muc's men killed most of the Americans at the radar trailers and were in control of the peak by 5 a.m. Still, they couldn't get a good enough angle of attack on the men in the alcove without exposing themselves to direct fire by the uninjured Etchberger. Five sappers were killed and a number of others were wounded while the North Vietnamese reported killing at least 10 Americans. Muc confirmed this after surveying the area.

At dawn Monday, March 11, Air America helicopter pilot Ken Wood and crew chief Rusty Irons, both 28, boarded a UH-1H Huey chopper at the CIA flying hub in Long Tieng, Laos. The men had worked with each other previously but weren't consistently assigned to fly together. Both were Army veterans who had already spent years in Southeast Asia. Wood, a Detroit native, was relatively new to the CIA, having left the military less than a year earlier with 1,000 hours of flying time in the region. Irons, who grew up in Southern California, had joined the CIA in 1965. In early 1968, it was customary for a single man to fly an Air America chopper, but a co-pilot was later often added after the war intensified. Crew chiefs like Irons were essential to any mission, and their duties went far beyond loading and unloading the aircraft: they were the eyes and ears for anything the pilots couldn't see or hear up front, and a strong bond existed between them. Like the Project Heavy Green men, Irons and Wood were assigned out of Udorn Air Base, and they knew about the radar mission atop Phou Pha Thi as each had previously flown resupply missions to Site 85. Irons, in fact, had been at the peak a day earlier with another pilot.

Rescue missions were a side job for Air America crews, who spent much of their time supplying Thai soldiers and Lao fighters. They also flew in support of U.S. Agency for International Development activities such as delivering food to rural areas. Irons didn't find rescue work particularly daunting as chopper crews rarely drew fire during such missions because they usually got to the site before the enemy. They were fired upon more often simply by crossing over places where rival forces just happened to be. Wood flew in southern Laos for a few months after joining Air America but didn't find it challenging enough, so he requested a transfer to Long Tieng so he could learn to fly in the mountains with the best pilots. Air America was a true brotherhood that featured a lot of healthy competition, he said.

"It's what kept you on your toes. You could always improve, but you felt like you had reached the pinnacle," said Wood. "On a scale of 1 to 10, everyone was a 9-plus. We became so finely tuned in our flying techniques it didn't get any better than that."

On this morning, he and Irons made a quick trip from Long Tieng to refuel at nearby Lima Site 36. While they were loading enough gas to fly for three hours, they heard some radio chatter about men in need of rescue. Wood turned on the chopper's automatic direction finder, which pointed straight to Phou Pha Thi. They looked across the valley 15 or 20 miles, saw smoke on the western side of a ridge and quickly decided to see if they could be of any help, estimating they could make it there in 15 minutes. Though several Air America and U.S. Air Force chopper crews responded, Wood and Irons were the first on scene equipped with a motorized winch and 200-plus feet of cable capable of lifting more than 500 pounds.

"I didn't go out there for adventure," Wood said. "I went out there to do a job. If I had not been the first one that got there, I'm sure that any other pilot would have gone in there."

He steered the aircraft to the peak and made radio contact with someone on the ground. It was John Daniel. Wood asked him if the men had any smoke to mark their location. Sliz had a canister in his survival vest, but his hands were injured and he couldn't engage it. Instead, Etchberger popped it and unleashed a purple cloud. By this time, it was 7:30 a.m.

At 5,800-foot elevation on the edge of a cliff, a helicopter with a full load of fuel made for tricky flying. Wood put the front of the rotor system over the ridge line, while Irons activated the winch and lowered a rescue cable toward the peak. Etchberger held off the enemy with gunfire as the pilot, guided by Irons, inched the chopper to the edge of the cliff. A dazed Sliz saw the rescue cable appear in front of him. At its end was a jungle penetrator, a 3-leaf steel device that opened like flower petals so a man could straddle it. Etchberger exposed himself to heavy enemy fire as he helped Daniel onto the apparatus.

"He told me, 'I'll be right up. I'll see you in a minute,'" said Daniel.

Irons whisked Daniel upward as Etchberger fired toward the NVA sappers. The crew chief then sent the cable back down, and Etchberger helped Sliz climb aboard. The cable swung out and slammed him back into the side of the mountain. Muc, the sapper commander, said one of his men was shot to death while trying to stop the rescue, and it's possible Etchberger did the killing as he was the lone American in this area still armed at this point. Irons, the chopper crew chief, was focused on reeling in the airmen and never fired his AK-47 rifle.

While being lifted toward the chopper, Sliz saw Staff Sgt. William Husband running across the peak toward the ledge. The young man had been playing dead nearby for hours. Sliz joined Daniel aboard the chopper. It was listing a bit, so Irons directed them to move to the other side to balance the load. He reversed the hoist to send it back for the other two men and glanced down to see Etchberger smashing his and Daniel's rifles against rocks to render them useless to the enemy. Husband was with him by this point and they clutched the cable together as Irons pulled them skyward with the winch. They made it safely aboard just as pilot Wood made the decision to pull away because the ground fire was so intense.

"I said, 'I don't have anyone else who can fly this machine (so) we need to get the hell out of here' and I backed off the ledge," Wood said. "(The rescue) probably took no longer than five minutes but at that time it seemed like an eternity. I was thinking, 'Hey, when's this going to be over with?'"

Irons moved his AK-47 firearm out of the way so Etchberger could sit on a bench seat next to him. Just then, a burst of gunfire from below surprised Irons and left four or five dime-sized holes in the floor. The crew chief was sitting on a flak vest and had positioned his toolbox under him for added protection from below. He noticed a bullet hole in the stock of his rifle and felt Etchberger lean against him. Irons was still experiencing an adrenaline rush and thought the airman was simply exhausted from his grueling experience. As Wood steered the chopper away from the mountain, Husband told him that Staff Sgt. Jack Starling, a tactical air navigation system maintainer, was injured on a different part of the peak and unable to move quickly. Wood immediately put that message out on the radio rescue channel. In the back of the Air America chopper, Irons noticed blood dripping on the floor underneath Etchberger. The 35-year-old senior noncommissioned officer had taken a single round into his rectum. Irons had a tiny first aid kit but no time or skill to do anything for the gravely injured man. He was dead or close to it when they landed at Site 36, just 35 minutes after Wood and Irons had departed the same airfield.

The rescue work wasn't yet done at Phou Pha Thi. In swooped an Air Force HH-3E Jolly Green Giant chopper flown by Capt. Russ Cayler and Capt. Joe Panza of Udorn's 40th Air Rescue and Recovery Service. Also aboard were a crew chief and two pararescue jumpers. These men had left Thailand before dawn, heading north across the

Mekong River to hook up with the Skyraiders. It was standard for two A-1 pilots to fly ahead of a rescue chopper to assess the situation, but Jolly Green Giant co-pilot Panza said all four Skyraider pilots may have gone ahead this time due to the seriousness of the attack. As his helicopter approached Phou Pha Thi from the west, the Skyraiders were already attacking. Panza watched the Air America chopper rescue of Etchberger, Sliz, Daniel and Husband unfold before hearing Wood on the radio say that an injured American was still on the peak. As Cayler steered the chopper closer, the men noticed a signal from a flashlight on the side of the mountain and figured correctly it was Starling trying to get their attention.

Armed with an M-16, pararescueman Sgt. James "JJ" Rogers was lowered to the peak by hoist and cable. He touched ground and clutched the cable so he would remain connected to the helicopter. He stumbled and dropped his rifle, which toppled out of reach. In the chopper, Panza looked down at the peak and saw numerous bodies, but he couldn't tell if they were those of Americans or the enemy. Starling, whose legs were injured, surprised Rogers by approaching him from behind and touching his shoulder. The pararescueman unfolded the arms of the jungle penetrator at the end of his cable, and the men climbed onto it as Cayler maneuvered away from the peak, the men dangling perhaps 200 feet below the aircraft—and a few thousand feet above the valley below—as they were reeled back toward it.

"They got the ride of their lives," said Panza.

The Jolly Green Giant headed for Site 36 behind the Air America Huey flown by Wood. Upon the lead chopper's arrival, Etchberger's body was put on a litter. It and the surviving airmen were quickly transferred to another aircraft and flown to Thailand. Irons and Wood immediately began assessing their chopper for damage. The rounds that came through the floor had come dangerously close to the flight controls. One had just missed a fuel line, while another had peeled back metal in the engine deck. The chopper had bigger holes elsewhere but was deemed flyable so the men were back in the air an hour or so later. They knew they had just participated in something remarkable, but it was still early in their workday and they had other tasks to accomplish before they could reflect on it.

The rescue work continued atop Phou Pha Thi, though. A second Jolly Green Giant piloted by Air Force Capt. Al Montrem landed at the heliport to pick up the forward air controller and CIA men Spence and Freeman. As he touched down, he was faced with throngs of Hmong guerillas and family members dashing toward the chopper. He rescued the CIA men and about 25 friendlies. At Udorn, Master Sgt. Frank Roura met the aircraft that carried his comrades. He was shaken to see that only four men had returned alive and heartbroken by the sight of the body of Etchberger, his friend and fellow senior NCO. Clayton went aboard and initially mistook Etchberger for another man on the crew.

"Everybody got off the plane and (I saw) there was a body laying on a stretcher in there. I went aboard the airplane and looked down," he said. "My first glance, I thought that was someone else – one of the other sergeants. And then I realized it was Dick. Wasn't a mark on him."

After the men were rescued, U.S. aircraft resumed air strikes on the peak, attempting to destroy the radar equipment, TACAN system and the 12.75-mm antiaircraft gun. Muc and his men collected weapons, equipment and documents. They found a few small arms and a large map torn into several pieces by an air strike. They were joined at some point by other NVA forces. Muc and his men spent that night on the mountain and left the morning of Tuesday, March 12, to return to North Vietnam, where the lieutenant presented a verbal report to his commander, saying that his men had killed all of the Americans at the site who were not rescued by air.

14

Ambassador Sullivan spent much of Monday, March 11, getting updates on the situation atop Phou Pha Thi and relaying that information by cable from the U.S. embassy in Vientiane to State Department headquarters in Washington, D.C.

> *As Depart has probably learned from military sources, enemy has effectively eliminated air navigation facilities at Site 85. Action began yesterday evening with artillery and mortar shelling. Decision to destroy facilities by self-destruction was taken in small hours of morning. Helicopter evacuation was arranged for first light this morning.*
>
> *Evacuation plans have been seriously disrupted by enemy activity and several . . . personnel have apparently been dispersed from pre-planned evacuation sites. Although seven of them have been accounted for as of this time, 11 are yet to be located. Of those accounted for, three are dead on the site, one died in the helicopter en route and three are at Udorn.*

The ambassador's numbering was a bit off since there were 16 Heavy Green men on the peak during the attack, as well as two CIA representatives and an Air Force forward air controller. Among the Americans reported dead on site were Hank Gish and Monk Springsteadah, the two killed on the ledge where they huddled with Sliz, Daniel and Etchberger, the one mentioned as dying in the chopper. The friendly 224-man local defense forces below the peak suffered eight killed, 18 missing and 33 wounded, the ambassador wrote.

In addition to these personnel, two (Continental Air Services men) and one (Air Force forward air controller) have been withdrawn from their evacuation sites. Other local personnel (wounded, etc.) have also been extracted.

Fighting and shelling continues, as well as helicopter and ground evacuation efforts. Because of confused situation at site and withdrawal of our CAS personnel (one of whom was wounded), it will doubtless be some time before we have (a) clear picture or further significant reports.

We will, of course, continue reports as information comes in. At first glance, however, it appears we may have pushed our luck one day too long in attempting to keep this facility in operation.

Three decades later, retired Air Force officer Tim Castle would use the phrase "one day too long" as the title for a book about Project Heavy Green's role in the North Vietnam bombing campaign.

Someone from the Air Force phoned Kay Etchberger the night of Tuesday, March 12 to tell her of her husband's death, just hours after she had learned that her first grandchild had been born in California. Rich, 10, answered the call as trained by his father, saying "Hello, Etchberger residence. Can I help you?" He handed the phone to his mother. Cory, 9, was at the dinner table when she took that second call, and he watched his mother collapse to the floor in anguish, screaming "They said they would not call! They said they would not call!"—but come in person—if something happened to her husband. Cory ran to a neighboring house to get help. Rich stayed with his mother, who didn't say anything about his father being dead until his brother returned with help. The boys' grandparents came over to the home. Rich remembers his grandfather's eyes being red from crying and that his grandmother never ceased weeping the whole time they were there.

In a March 13 cable, Sullivan said evacuation operations of friendly forces had been completed and that the site was then in enemy hands.

Final count on . . . personnel accounts for all but three. One of these may subsequently be listed as dead if and when we can get more coherent information from survivors, some of whom (are) in state of considerable shock.

Aside from the three confirmed killed, the bodies of nine missing Air Force men weren't recovered from the site, leading to speculation— including by some of their loved ones—that perhaps at least some of them had been taken prisoner. A quarter-century later, Muc said it wasn't so. It was the flying service's greatest loss of ground personnel in the war. Sullivan's telegram acknowledged that 16 Air Force men were present and five were extracted alive, but Etchberger was killed in a helicopter when he was hit by ground fire. Eight others were known dead. Three were unaccounted for, "although none of them . . . may be presumed dead," wrote Sullivan, who said confusion surrounding the extraction stemmed from two factors not yet fully explained: first, that the men, instead of assembling at a pre-arranged evacuation site—the helipad near the CIA site— "decided to climb down over the face of sheer cliffs to a narrow ledge."

> It is not known why or when they decided to take this action. But it is presumed that they must have thought, contrary to fact, that trail to evacuation site was blocked.
>
> Second (factor) was (the) fact that a small enemy "suicide squad," which seems to have made improbable ascent up these same cliffs, surprised and caught these . . . personnel on their narrow ledge, gunning and grenading them while they were trapped in this inescapable position. It was here that (these men) suffered such heavy casualties and where most of them are reported to have died. Three bodies were subsequently seen on this ledge, but remainder are assumed to have fallen off sheer 2,000-foot drop.

Some of these details would later prove to be untrue or at least not wholly accurate. The recovery mission claimed another life when pilot Capt. Donald Westbrook's A-1E Skyraider was shot down March 12 as he looked for survivors. The ambassador's cable said the Air Force flew several missions that day to destroy equipment on the peak. Photo missions were scheduled March 13 to determine whether more strikes were necessary. Sullivan said he would make that decision based on discussions with 7th Air Force/13th Air Force leaders and planned to talk to the Royal Lao Government to determine what, if anything, needed to be said about the attack. A footnote on this transcript says that he informed Prince Souvanna Phouma about the battle, and that survivors said the three unaccounted-for men had, in fact, been killed. It remained to be seen whether or not Hanoi or Pathet Lao leaders would announce their victory. The ambassador said his staff and Air Force personnel at Udorn Air Base would continue to reconstruct the attack with details from survivors when they recovered from sedation and shock.

> *Conclusion, however, seems quite definitive that none of missing personnel (is) likely to be alive. We must decide how to handle next of kin notification, casualty announcements, etc. We must expedite action for replacement site, at least for TACAN (the tactical air navigation system).*

Sullivan makes no mention of restarting Project Heavy Green in a new location. No ground counterattack was possible by friendly forces due to the overwhelming size of enemy fighters in the region. There was no alternative but to evacuate foreign friendly troops and their dependents to maintain them intact for counterattack activity in the upcoming rainy season, the ambassador said. North Vietnam had mounted an offensive of this scale because it wished to eliminate U.S. presence on the peak, which had become an "attractive nuisance for them," he noted. "Consequently, this vast uprooting of human resources and abandonment of useful territory is direct result (of) U.S. rather than Royal Lao Government interests."

Sullivan wondered whether the enemy would attempt an attack on nearby Site 36. Though it was more heavily defended than Site 85, "it is questionable whether it can withstand a determined assault by seven (North Vietnamese) battalions, the strength we feel (the) enemy is probably able to deploy against it." Lao military commander Gen. Vang Pao messaged Sullivan and Souvanna asking for maximum air strikes against targets in or near population centers. They agreed to have U.S. photo interpreters examine them for opportunities and later met with Lao generals to discuss objectives, with Sullivan insisting that Souvanna personally accept responsibility for the targeting.

John Daniel and Stan Sliz didn't know Dick Etchberger had been killed until they awoke at the Udorn Air Base dispensary in Thailand. The information stunned Daniel as Etchberger was the only one of the three who had survived at the cliff who hadn't been injured before boarding the helicopter. Sliz awoke initially to find a doctor digging in his thigh. "What the fuck are you doing?" he screamed. A nurse held up a piece of shrapnel and said, "He was digging this fucking thing out of you" before Sliz passed out again.

Clayton, the mission commander, found Sliz incoherent on his first visit to the hospitalized officer and later debriefed him as he received treatment at the 100-bed medical facility at Camp Friendship adjacent to Korat Air Base, Thailand. When Sliz came to for good, he was the target of a tirade by Staff Sgt. Jack Starling, who blamed Sliz for leaving him behind on the peak, presumably because he was one of the commissioned officers in charge of the mission. Clayton talked to others who survived the attack, including CIA staffer Howard Freeman, who had been shot in the leg during a skirmish near the CIA trailers. Clayton then accompanied Etchberger's body back to Hamburg, his Pennsylvania hometown, via a series of flights on Air Force transport and refueling airplanes. At Clark Air Base, he spoke about the attack with 13th Air Force Commander Lt. Gen. Benjamin O. Davis Jr.

"When I finished, he came around the desk, shook my hand and said, 'Colonel, when you've finished with this, I want you to go home and see your family,'" said Clayton.

At Yokota Air Base, Japan, a colonel told Clayton, who was wearing a flightsuit with no insignia on it, that he needed to commandeer the KC-135 Stratotanker containing the bodies of Etchberger and other fallen GIs to return with it to his stateside unit. This meant the dozens of bodies on it would need to be transferred to another plane. Clayton said it wasn't possible and called the Pentagon's special operations' staff to tell them what the man wanted. They handled it from there.

"About an hour later, this colonel comes walking up to me again and says, 'Mister, I don't know who the hell you are but we'll meet again sometime," said Clayton.

Before Clayton arrived in the United States, the Pentagon had sent a press release about Etchberger's death "in a helicopter crash" in Southeast Asia to the *Hamburg Item*, which printed the notice in its March 16 edition. After delivering the body, he lingered for a short time in the historic downtown, venturing down Fourth Street from the Burkey and Spacht

Funeral Home to Miller's 5 & 10 where Etchberger had worked as a teen and that his father still managed at age 60. Clayton's superiors had told him not to engage anyone and, anyway, he didn't have the heart to enter the store. He soon caught a ride to Washington, D.C., with an employee of the funeral home, spending time there with his own family and visiting the Pentagon to talk about the collapse of Project Heavy Green.

Even before she buried her husband's body, Kay Etchberger started to let his closest pals from the service know that he had been killed. She drafted a letter to Technical Sgt. Ed Perrigo, who had served under her husband in the Philippines and had since been reassigned to Michigan. Kay didn't know him well, having only had brief conversations with him when he stopped by their home near Clark Air Base. She knew he was close to her husband, though.

"She recognized our relationship, and that's why she opted to write me directly and tell me because she knew that I would experience a loss," Perrigo said.

She told him about her husband's death in a March 15 note, also mentioning the charcoal rubbings Dick had made of a Thai temple for him. Etch had mailed them to her with directions to forward them to his friend.

Dear Ed,

> *This is so hard for me to write, but being the friend you were to Dick, I must. Dick was killed in Southeast Asia on March 10. They had been under heavy ground fire all night, when daylight came they flew in a helicopter to take them out. They made it in but were hit by ground fire on takeoff. When they got to the base, Dick was gone.*
>
> *This is all like a dream, Ed, but I had just received your temple rubbings, and I will see you get them. God does strange things. The same day, Dick became a grandfather. Steve is at Norton AFB and they had a baby girl.*

Kay

Dick Etchberger's body was buried March 22, 1968, in a cemetery adjacent to his former high school. Since his 1951 graduation, it had been converted to an elementary school campus where his two younger sons attended classes. Students and teachers watched the service from the other side of a fence and heard the shots of a 21-gun salute. Steve Wilson couldn't attend his stepfather's funeral as he was home in California with his wife and newborn daughter.

On March 27, Ambassador Sullivan sent a note to Gen. William W. Momyer, commander of 7th Air Force/13th Air Force, saying that a "post mortem" of the loss of Lima Site 85 was needed if the general believed that a relatively small force had sacked the peak.

> *Our intelligence indicates their numbers between five and seven battalions, with artillery and rocket support, considerably outnumbering local defense forces, which never numbered more than 1,000 men in (the) 12-kilometer defensive perimeter drawn around Site 85.*
>
> *We made clear from the very beginning that this site could not be defended against a determined and superior enemy force. We gave regular and accurate estimates of its progressive deterioration and, as early as February 26, advised you that it could probably not be held beyond March 10. Therefore, its fall should have come as no surprise to anyone.*

What should be studied, Sullivan said, with a view to future operations was how the enemy's artillery fire was surprisingly accurate from a considerable distance.

> *It seems possible that installations were rendered effectively inoperable even before destruction order was given. There may be some lessons in this which should be studied with respect to length of time technical personnel should be required (to) stay at their posts after installation falls within artillery range. In hindsight, it seems to me we should have pulled all technicians out morning (of) March 10 even if this meant losing the last several hours of the installation's capabilities.*

Sullivan spent the rest of the cable wondering why some men had sought shelter at the cliff instead of going to the helipad at the CIA portion of the peak. More than two weeks after the attack, he apparently still didn't grasp that it was only about a third of the men who did that and had done so as it was opposite from where the early artillery fire had come. Nearly all of the others were in the trailers until the North Vietnamese special forces surprised them there.

> *It is still not clear why technical personnel went over cliff to a narrow ledge rather than down trail to chopper pad. (Continental Air Services) and local personnel subsequently went up same trail to installation searching for technicians, so we know trail was traversable, even if under artillery fire. It is also not clear to me how (a) small Vietnamese suicide squad got to installation site, although it seems they must have scaled the cliff, which all of us considered impassable.*

In a March 30 memo to new Defense Secretary Clark Clifford, Army Gen. Earle G. Wheeler, who had returned to his post as chairman of the Joint Chiefs of Staff following the heart attack he'd suffered the previous summer, described how the communists used the eastern panhandle of Laos as a sanctuary and had developed a logistic and troop movement system—the Ho Chi Minh Trail—to South Vietnam through that area. The enemy's Tet offensive was supported in large measure through the Lao panhandle, he noted.

> *Regular NVA units are being employed in offensive operations against Royal Lao Government forces. Generally, the U.S. Government has adhered to a policy of respect for the Geneva Agreements and has undertaken military actions in Laos only in response to mounting North Vietnamese violations. These military actions have been generally of low intensity and have been conducted largely with the knowledge and consent of the Royal Laotian Government. Further, these military actions have been planned and executed carefully in order to preserve the fragile political balance of power in Laos to avoid public exposure and to minimize the likelihood of communist takeover of the entire country. So long as North Vietnam controls eastern Laos, attainment of U.S. objectives in Southeast Asia will be most difficult.*

The Joint Chiefs of Staff forwarded a draft memo to Secretary of State Dean Rusk expressing concern over the gravity of the situation in Laos, proposing formal consideration of the problem by the government's Interdepartmental Regional Group/East Asia or other appropriate panel. Around the same time, a Special National Intelligence Estimate had gauged communist intentions in Laos for the ensuing few months and included reference to the loss of Site 85.

On March 31, President Lyndon B. Johnson told a nationwide TV audience that he would not seek re-election that fall, though up to that point his address had focused almost solely on the war and included a denouncement of any purported communist successes in the Tet Offensive. He reiterated the terms of America's offer from six months earlier to negotiate with the North Vietnamese with one remarkable change: he agreed to stop bombing in most areas of the North to coax communist leaders to the bargaining table.

> *Tonight, I renew the offer I made last August: to stop the bombardment of North Vietnam. We ask that talks begin promptly, that they be serious talks on the substance of peace. We assume that, during those talks, Hanoi will not take advantage of our restraint.*
>
> *We are prepared to move immediately toward peace through negotiations. So, tonight, in the hope that this action will lead to early talks, I am taking the first step to deescalate the conflict. We are reducing—substantially reducing—the present level of hostilities. And we are doing so unilaterally, and at once.*
>
> *Tonight, I have ordered our aircraft and our naval vessels to make no attacks on North Vietnam, except in the area north of the demilitarized zone where the continuing enemy buildup directly threatens allied forward positions and where the movements of their troops and supplies are clearly related to that threat. The area in which we are stopping our attacks includes almost 90 percent of North Vietnam's population and most of its territory. Thus, there will be no attacks around the principal populated areas or in the food-producing areas of North Vietnam.*
>
> *Even this very limited bombing of the North could come to an early end if our restraint is matched by restraint in Hanoi. But I cannot in good conscience stop all bombing so long as to do so would immediately and directly endanger the lives of our*

men and our allies. Whether a complete bombing halt becomes possible in the future will be determined by events.

Our purpose in this action is to bring about a reduction in the level of violence that now exists.

It is to save the lives of brave men, and to save the lives of innocent women and children. It is to permit the contending forces to move closer to a political settlement. We have no intention of widening this war. But the United States will never accept a fake solution to this long and arduous struggle and call it peace.

No one can foretell the precise terms of an eventual settlement.

Our objective in South Vietnam has never been the annihilation of the enemy. It has been to bring about a recognition in Hanoi that its objective—taking over the South by force—could not be achieved.

Peace will come because Asians were willing to work for it—and to sacrifice for it—and to die by the thousands for it. But let it never be forgotten: Peace will come also because America sent her sons to help secure it.

It has not been easy—far from it. During the past 4½ years, it has been my fate and my responsibility to be commander-in-chief. I have lived—daily and nightly—with the cost of this war. I know the pain that it has inflicted. I know, perhaps better than anyone, the misgivings that it has aroused.

Throughout this entire, long period, I have been sustained by a single principle: that what we are doing now, in Vietnam, is vital not only to the security of Southeast Asia, but it is vital to the security of every American.

I believe that a peaceful Asia is far nearer to reality because of what America has done in Vietnam. I believe that the men who endure the dangers of battle—fighting there for us tonight—are helping the entire world avoid far greater conflicts, far wider wars, far more destruction, than this one.

The peace that will bring them home someday will come. Tonight I have offered the first in what I hope will be a series of mutual moves toward peace. I pray that it will not be rejected by the leaders of North Vietnam. I pray that they will accept it as a means by which the sacrifices of their own people may be ended. And I ask your help and your support, my fellow citizens, for this effort to reach across the battlefield toward an early peace.

The ultimate strength of our country and our cause will lie not in powerful weapons or infinite resources or boundless wealth, but will lie in the unity of our people.

Johnson then shifted into talking about how partisan politics wasn't healthy for the progress of the nation.

What we won when all of our people united must not now be lost in suspicion, distrust, selfishness and politics among any of our people.

Believing this as I do, I have concluded that I should not permit the presidency to become involved in the partisan divisions that are developing in this political year.

With America's sons in the fields far away, with America's future under challenge right here at home, with our hopes and the world's hopes for peace in the balance every day, I do not believe that I should devote an hour or a day of my time to any personal partisan causes or to any duties other than the awesome duties of this office—the presidency of your country.

Accordingly, I shall not seek, and I will not accept, the nomination of my party for another term as your president.

But let men everywhere know, however, that a strong, a confident, and a vigilant America stands ready tonight to seek an honorable peace—and stands ready tonight to defend an honored cause—whatever the price, whatever the burden, whatever the sacrifice that duty may require.

Around the time of the president's announcement, Jerry Clayton returned to Thailand and what was left of his team. He and his superiors discussed finding another location to resume the radar mission but ultimately decided against it, and the project officially ground to a halt. Frank Roura remembers the despair he and his comrades felt in the weeks after the attack.

"We knew people had been there, our live friends, who were no longer there and there is nothing we (could) do about it," he said. "What the hell can you say or do? You can't go in (and) do something because there was nothing we could do. Our morale was nothing. Absolutely zero."

Roura closed up shop with Maj. Don Lehman, the radar controller whose men were sent to the hill without him by Clayton the day before the attack. At the commander's behest, Roura drafted a recommendation for Etchberger to receive the Medal of Honor based on interviews the men did with the survivors. It read:

> *CMSgt. Richard L. Etchberger distinguished himself by extraordinary heroism in connection with military operations against an opposing force as Radar Maintenance Superintendent, Detachment 1, 1043 Radar Evaluation Squadron, Headquarters Command, United States Air Force, while serving with friendly foreign forces engaged in armed conflict against an opposing armed force on *12 March 1968. On that date, CMSgt. Etchberger was with his unit in a defensive position at an operating location in Southeast Asia when the site was attacked by an overwhelming enemy ground force. The defensive position, having been chosen because of its invulnerability against artillery and mortar attack which had been in progress for over seven hours, became untenable under ground attack. The enemy was able to deliver sustained and withering fire on CMSgt. Etchberger's position from above. He returned fire with such intensity that the enemy force was repulsed. During this action, CMSgt. Etchberger continued to call for air rescue on his survival radio. His two surviving companions, Capt. Stanley J. Sliz and Staff Sgt. John G. Daniel, were seriously wounded, and when the rescue helicopter arrived, he exposed himself to enemy fire while placing and securing each injured man on the rescue sling. He delivered fire with one arm while using the other arm to carry and secure each man to the sling thus permitting them to be safely delivered to the helicopter. He was then hoisted to the rescue aircraft and as he reached the sill of the helicopter, he was*

---

* The attack happened overnight March 10-11, 1968.

fatally wounded by ground fire. His fierce defense, culminating in the supreme sacrifice of his life, saved the lives of his two fellow airmen. Through his extraordinary heroism, superb marksmanship and aggressiveness, CMSgt. Etchberger reflected the highest credit upon himself and the United States Air Force.

Roura forwarded it to higher headquarters and left Thailand to join his family in Oregon. The Heavy Green men who weren't on Phou Pha Thi during the attack returned to the United States. Each visited Lockheed's operation in Ontario, California, to make a statement and then traveled to the Pentagon for debriefing. They were officially accepted back into the Air Force and instructed to never talk about the mission, not even to each other. None directly returned to his former unit.

"We were scattered all over the United States. In fact, all over the world," said Roura.

Though his description of Etchberger's actions was largely accurate, his friend was not going to receive the Medal of Honor anytime soon. In fact, his remarkable actions remained largely unknown for decades even within the Air Force. The men he rescued couldn't even talk about what he'd done to preserve their lives.

After undergoing several operations in Southeast Asia, Capt. Stan Sliz was sent in April 1968 to a hospital in Illinois, his native state, which he had designated his "home of record" for military purposes. That decision wasn't the best because his wife, Ann, and children were in North Dakota, where they'd been stationed for several years prior to him being tapped for Project Heavy Green. Ann Sliz loaded up their children and drove to Illinois. She agonized over seeing him on crutches as he waited outside of the hospital for them and was dismayed to see the extent of his wounds while changing dressings on his legs when they visited his parents in Chicago. He was discharged from the hospital in June and reported to duty that summer at Hickam Air Force Base, Hawaii, where he worked in base operations and at the command post.

Staff Sgt. John Daniel remained in a Colorado hospital for more than a year after returning from Southeast Asia. He was then assigned to a teaching position at Keesler Air Force Base, Mississippi. Sliz and

Daniel suffered from their wounds, both physically and mentally, for decades to come.

Their commander, Clayton, was tormented by the loss of his men and the mission's collapse. He harbored no belief that any Americans had survived the attack and was troubled that the United States didn't have bodies to return to grieving families. At some point he heard that a French news photographer had visited Phou Pha Thi in the aftermath of the attack and had pictures of American bodies. He was willing to go to Europe to track down this man but his superiors rejected the idea, he said. He settled into a new special operations assignment at the Pentagon in mid-1968 and did what he could to have Etchberger considered for the Medal of Honor. Eventually, he received word that his fallen compatriot would receive the Air Force Cross, the service's second-highest award, because presenting a greater decoration could attract attention to U.S. presence in Laos. Air Force Chief of Staff Gen. John P. McConnell told him the service would upgrade the medal "when the time comes."

"(He said) this is too touchy for him to get the Medal of Honor now. Politically, it's dynamite," said Clayton. "Here we are with armed people out of uniform in Laos and (we're saying) there aren't any Americans there. Nothing like this had ever happened in the covert operations business. The main (post-attack) effort went into making sure that our operation was not compromised."

An Air Force Cross ceremony was set at the Pentagon for January 1969, the same month that President Johnson's administration gave way to that of Richard M. Nixon. It had been 10 months since the attack in Laos. Clayton met Kay Etchberger, her school-age sons, and Dick's parents, brother and uncle. Her son, Steven, was released from his job as an Air Force transport mechanic in California to attend the ceremony. The young airman was alarmed to find himself rubbing elbows with generals and Chief Master Sgt. of the Air Force Paul W. Airey, the top enlisted man in his service. It was the first time he had seen his mother and brothers since his stepfather's death.

If any of Etchberger's survivors didn't know the true story of his final actions beforehand, they did when the wording accompanying award of the decoration was read at the ceremony. There was no mention of a helicopter crash, because it hadn't happened. In fact, the text was virtually identical to what Roura had drafted the previous spring in Thailand. Reiterating what he had earlier said to Clayton, General McConnell told Kay Etchberger and her brother-in-law, Robert, that the award would be upgraded to the Medal of Honor when it wasn't such a hot issue politically.

In the years to come, Kay Etchberger maintained a predictable routine in Pennsylvania for the sake of Rich and Cory. When her in-laws moved from Hamburg to neighboring Edenburg, she bought a new home there for her and the boys. She received $70,000 from a life insurance policy provided by Lockheed and earned death benefits from the military. Her husband's time away from the service while working in Southeast Asia was nullified by the filing of a form stating that any other document saying his enlistment had ended in fall 1967 was an error. Though signed by Etchberger before his departure from the U.S., it was dated March 10, 1968—his last full day alive—by someone in Washington after word reached the Pentagon that he had been killed.

Kay had enjoyed being an Air Force wife for 11 years, but didn't make any outward move to keep a connection to the military. She rarely spoke of her husband's death in Laos, except to those family members and friends closest to her. As far as anyone else knew, he had died in a helicopter crash in Southeast Asia just like the *Hamburg Item* said he had. The family never pressured service leaders into honoring McConnell's Medal of Honor promises and, as happens in the military, the people in charge then weren't around long before retiring or moving on to other assignments. McConnell served as the Air Force's top general just six months past the Air Force Cross ceremony, retiring in July 1969 and being succeeded by his deputy, Gen. John D. Ryan, who knew about Project Heavy Green and Site 85 from his previous assignment as head of Pacific Air Forces. Etchberger's actions, as well as the memory of Project Heavy Green, faded even as talk about America's involvement in Laos grew.

On March 6, 1970, two years after the Phou Pha Thi attack, President Nixon issued a lengthy statement regarding American operations in Laos during his administration and those of Presidents Johnson and Kennedy. He said the United States had no ground combat forces in Laos and had only provided logistical and other assistance to the Lao government for the purpose of helping it prevent a communist conquest. Nixon seems to have been splitting hairs by saying the U.S. had no "ground combat" forces in Laos. America had ground forces there previously, if not when he spoke, and they had engaged in combat even though it wasn't their primary role. Later in the same statement, he declared that "no American stationed in Laos has ever been killed in ground combat operations." While airmen at Site 85 weren't typical ground troops, they were American GIs armed with M-16s who were in a battle with North Vietnamese Army special forces. An argument that they weren't in the military during their time in Laos is a pale one as they were readily readmitted to the Air Force immediately upon the collapse of their mission there. Nixon said the United States had used air power to interrupt the flow of North Vietnamese troops and supplies on the part of the Ho Chi Minh Trail that runs through Laos and, at the request of the Royal Lao government, had flown reconnaissance missions in Northern Laos in support of the nation's efforts to defend itself against North Vietnamese aggression. He acknowledged that the United States was engaged in "some other activities."

> *In recent days, however, there has been intense public speculation to the effect that the United States' involvement in Laos has substantially increased in violation of the Geneva accords, that American ground forces are engaged in combat in Laos, and that our air activity has had the effect of escalating the conflict.*

Nixon said there were no American ground forces in Laos and the nation had no plans to introduce any there. The U.S. government directly employed 616 Americans in Laos, he said, and 424 U.S. citizens were employed on contract to the government or to its subcontractors. Of these 1,040 Americans, the total number of GIs and civilians engaged in a military advisory or training capacity numbered 390, while logistics personnel numbered 323, the president said.

Ten days after Nixon's comments about Laos, the *Washington Post* ran a largely accurate story about the Phou Pha Thi attack by reporter T.D. Allman. Around the general time of Nixon's remarks, Jerry Clayton and Stan Sliz were summoned to give testimony to a Senate subcommittee looking into U.S. involvement in Laos. Sliz made a statement that was forwarded to the committee, headed by Missouri Sen. Stuart Symington, who had been the first secretary of the Air Force a quarter-century earlier. Sliz was never asked to appear publicly.

When he finished his Pentagon duty, Clayton was selected to go back to the 1st Combat Evaluation Group headquarters in Louisiana to run its radar bomb scoring mission. It was his life's dream, but it didn't happen. He believed the commander there told officials at Strategic Air Command headquarters, its parent entity at Offutt Air Force Base, Nebraska, that he "was too hard to handle."

"Perhaps so. Worse things have been said about me," said Clayton. "When all is said and done, the truth is that I had the privilege and honor of serving with the most capable, hardworking and loyal people in the Air Force."

Clayton soon retired from the military. From time to time, he tried to jumpstart the Medal of Honor process for Etchberger, but he never made any real progress in the stifling bureaucracy of the Department of Defense. It would take the rising popularity of the Internet years in the future before any real progress was made to recognize his comrade. Even then, Clayton wasn't to be the driving factor in the award discussion reaching a high enough level for anything to happen.

Kay Etchberger never remarried. Her sons don't recall her ever dating anyone in the decades after her husband's death. She was a very positive person who made friends as easily in Pennsylvania as she had in the various military assignments on which she accompanied her husband. Kay took Rich and Cory on trips to see their relatives in Utah every other year, but there was never a doubt that she would continue to raise them in Pennsylvania because it was the best way to keep her late husband a part of their sons' lives. Their grandfather and uncle spent time with the boys, as did some of Etchberger's childhood pals. She and her sons stayed in the Hamburg area even after her mother-in-law died in 1972 at age 68.

Other than being the only children in town who had a parent killed in the Vietnam War, the Etchberger boys have good memories of growing up in Berks County. As teens, they owned minibikes and played tennis at Hamburg High, from which Rich graduated in 1976, followed a year later by Cory. Both attended college, eventually earning doctorate degrees and embarking on teaching careers. Their mother remained in the east until after her father-in-law's death in 1985 at age 77. By that time, the Air Force had declassified many details about Project Heavy Green. Someone from the Pentagon contacted Kay Etchberger and sent her a copy of an August 1968 report, *The Fall of Site 85,* prepared by the Contemporary Historical Examination of Current Operations (CHECO) division of the Tactical Evaluation Directorate at Pacific Air Forces headquarters in Hawaii. She finally had something concrete she could share with her grown sons . . . but she didn't. Her sons believe their mother may still have been uncomfortable talking about Project Heavy Green since she had promised not to in 1967.

Information began to trickle out to the public, though. In July 1986, Site 85 battle survivor William Husband agreed to do an in-person interview with prospective screenwriter Donald Metzger, a retired Air Force officer, at a hotel in Albuquerque, New Mexico. The transcript of that interview has been widely circulated among Project Heavy Green researchers and surviving family members. Clayton, though, regretted for years that it even existed. In it, Metzger said he had researched the mission for four years, interviewed 43 people and made 28 Freedom of Information Act requests for information from the federal government. Husband said he'd had no contact with any Heavy Green teammates since the mission collapsed 18 years earlier, and this was the first time anyone had asked him about what he saw during the attack. Metzger's transcript provides the only available comments from a Heavy Green man who survived the battle other than those made by Sliz, Daniel and Starling. Sliz and Daniel only saw what happened at their location at the cliff. Starling and Husband witnessed at least some of what happened at the trailers, though they sometimes contradict themselves in what they recalled. Husband's comments to Metzger about the actions of others during the attack seem believable because he criticizes himself as being ineffective.

Husband was a power production specialist, an essential part of the team who maintained the diesel-fueled generators that provided electricity to run the radar and TACAN systems. Husband, who has since died, had vivid memories of the attack. After the first rocket hit the camp, others flew overhead harmlessly. Team members divided up

M-16s, extra ammunition, grenades and survival vests. There weren't enough rifles for each man, but Blanton had a pistol, as did Tech Sgt. Herbert A. Kirk, a teletype maintenance specialist, he said. Husband may have confused Kirk with Springsteadah as multiple men confirmed that the latter had smuggled a personal sidearm with him from the United States. Husband was impressed with the confidence exhibited by Etchberger and Master Sgt. James Calfee, the mission's two senior NCOs. On this night, Calfee told the men to "remember fields of fire—don't shoot in directions of each other" while Etchberger said plainly that if the men needed to use the rifles, they should shoot to kill.

"(Etchberger) was our solid type of guy. He never seemed to worry and kept assuring us that it would be alright," Husband told Metzger.

The first rocket had blown holes in their living quarters, so Husband hid near the generators in a rock cutout big enough for one man. Calfee, Kirk, Starling, Blanton, Tech Sgt. Pat Shannon, Staff Sgt. Don Worley and Sgt. David Price were on duty inside the operations building. Tech Sgt. Mel Holland, Staff Sgt. James W. Davis and Tech Sgt. Willis R. Hall were in the living quarters for part of the time and then in the maintenance area, Husband said. Etchberger, Sliz, Daniel, Gish and Springsteadah were in hiding at the cliff.

Small-arms fire erupted after midnight but it was far enough away that the men on duty stayed at their positions in the operations trailer. Around 2 a.m., Husband went to the bunkroom. Price, Shannon and Calfee were in there. Husband said Daniel was there, but Daniel recalls being in the rock alcove with Etchberger and the others at this time of night. Calfee was calm, Husband said, but the others were agitated. Husband went back to the maintenance trailer and heard continuing gunfire in the distance. Based on direction from Sliz, Gish came to the maintenance trailer some time later to retrieve more ammunition and told the men there where he and the others on Sliz's crew were hiding.

"I hope I see you in the morning," said Gish, clearly disconcerted.

Husband checked on the generators at 2:45 a.m. and retreated to his solo hiding place after a rocket hit near the sleeping trailer. He soon heard men speaking a foreign language and walked toward the maintenance trailer to investigate. He saw men in uniforms and thought they were Hmong friendlies until they began shooting. His recollection disagreed somewhat from that of the sapper commander, Truong Muc. Blanton,

Calfee and Shannon walked out of the operations building with their arms raised, he said. Blanton tried showing something—perhaps his Lockheed employee ID card—to an enemy soldier. The man lowered his gun as Blanton approached but then raised it and opened fire on him, Shannon and Calfee, all of whom fell to the ground. Other men ran out of the trailers. Holland, the teletype man, was shot in an arm and fell. Kirk and Davis were shot but were able to crawl behind rocks by the maintenance building. Starling fired at the attackers. Husband and Davis went to Holland, who was screaming in pain. They told him to keep quiet or they'd all be killed. Price came over and said the men should head down the path toward the CIA trailer and helipad. Husband, stunned by a grenade, saw two enemy soldiers approaching him both get shot, possibly by Calfee.

Husband saw the bodies of Shannon and Tech Sgt. Herb Kirk and believed both to be dead, though he didn't stop to check. Kirk had been hit in the face and Shannon was missing an arm. This may be a mistake as another man reported that Kirk was the one missing an arm. Husband heard shooting from the direction of where Etchberger, Sliz and the other three men were hiding, but he didn't see anything that occurred there. He moved east and saw Price holding his arm but walking and trying to pull Holland's body. The teletype man was unconscious and probably dead, he thought. Husband never saw Tech Sgt. Willis Hall once the shooting began at the trailers. Husband saw enemy fire in the direction of Holland and Davis and later got close enough to see that neither was moving.

At daylight, A-1E Skyraider pilots arrived to provide fire support. The Air America helicopter flown by Ken Wood arrived on scene, and Husband looked up to see crew chief Rusty Irons lower a cable toward the cliff. He saw someone being pulled by winch to the chopper and dashed toward the ledge, passing the injured Starling, who pleaded with Husband to tell the pilot that he was there but couldn't move due to an injured leg. Husband sprinted to the ledge, where he found only Etchberger waiting. The two men rode up the cable together. Husband told the pilot that Starling was still alive, but Wood was already pulling away by that point due to enemy fire. One of those rounds came through the chopper's underside, fatally wounding Etchberger. Wood radioed other crews in the area that Starling needed help.

Husband recovered from his injuries at Clark Air Base in the Philippines. Frank Roura visited him to take a statement about Etchberger's actions. Husband spoke to Starling after their separate rescues and told Donald Metzger, during the 1986 interview, that Starling said he'd seen Calfee—hit in the face and upper chest—continue to fire at the enemy until he was mortally wounded. Starling also told Husband that Hall had died with Holland. Husband's account seems like an honest retelling of what he believed happened since he chastises himself for not fighting back.

"I was no hero. I never even fired my rifle. But the others did. Some didn't panic," said Husband. "I did what I did to survive, and sometimes I wish I would have died on the mountain with the others. I didn't act like I should have acted. I could have helped in the shooting, but I just didn't. I was afraid that if I shot, they would shoot back. I guess in a way I was a coward. I'm not afraid to admit that today. Maybe being a coward allowed me to live."

In 1986, the United States opened a small office in Ho Chi Minh City, formerly Saigon, as an initial step to improving relations between American and Vietnam as a way of finding information on more than 2,000 Americans missing in Southeast Asia. It launched its first research operation the next year, and the team started excavating various sites in the region in 1989. In 1990, Defense Intelligence Agency staffer Robert Destatte joined the effort. The retired Army warrant officer served three tours of duty in Vietnam during a 20-year career, married a woman from the country, and speaks Vietnamese fluently. He stayed in Hanoi for four years and said the countries had developed a congenial relationship into matters of missing U.S. service members by 1993.

"It was one of the highlights of my career," said Destatte. "Everything I did in service up to that point was to get me ready for this job."

Toward the end of his time in Southeast Asia, Destatte learned of an NBC TV news team visiting the region to report on Project Heavy Green. The broadcast journalism crew was accompanied by Clayton and Dr. Tim Castle, the retired Air Force officer conducting research for his book. The team conducted videotaped interviews in the United States with Stan Sliz, though he didn't travel to Asia. The news crew, Clayton and Castle visited Phou Pha Thi. Destatte met them afterward for drinks in a Ho Chi Minh City bar and saw unedited video of their trip. Years later, Clayton expressed frustration with his visit to the peak.

He had hoped that returning there might help identify what happened to his men.

"I think I was allowed to spend a total of about 20 minutes up there. That night I tried to talk to some of the missing persons' people (to tell them to look down the cliff), and NBC said, 'No, that's not part of what we've got you here for.' I should have told them then to kiss my rear end," said Clayton.

He met a North Vietnamese official in charge of POW/MIA affairs and asked him for information on where the bodies of his men were.

"While I was shaking his hand, he said, 'Colonel, you are trying to find the status of 11 people. I'm trying to determine the status of 700,000 people.' Boy, that gets your attention."

Destatte of the local POW/MIA office later visited Phou Pha Thi on at least two occasions. On one of these trips, he was accompanied by retired North Vietnamese Army Lt. Col. Truong Muc, who commanded the special forces unit that attacked the radar site a quarter-century earlier. Clayton also had met Muc, but questioned if he'd really been in charge of that operation or was a plant from the Vietnamese government because he didn't remember details of the attack and said his men didn't do anything with the bodies of the Americans. Destatte has no such reservations about Muc, whom he interviewed in January 1994. He told Destatte that he and his surviving men left the peak shortly after the attack and let a contingent of North Vietnamese Army soldiers decide what to do next. The officers of this larger NVA group looked around a bit to gather intelligence and left enlisted men in charge of disposing of the Americans' bodies. They simply threw them off of the cliff, Muc said. Destatte believes the unaccounted for men were all killed and their bodies disposed of this way because the peak doesn't have enough soil for burial, and it wasn't realistic for enemy soldiers to bring bodies down the hill with them.

"Things came into focus with Muc's input. While the sappers carried out the attack, regular NVA forces attacked the base of hill," said Destatte. "He said, 'These guys (the Americans) gave as good as they got.' His men took some casualties. (The Americans) had every reason to believe their position was secure from this kind of attack."

Destatte interviewed NVA officers who described where the bodies were when they arrived at the peak. POW/MIA task force members took three life-sized dummies and tossed them off the peak in different locations to see where they landed. Men then rappelled down to inspect those areas. This was an early step in what eventually led to the discovery of bone fragments from two of the missing Americans. Destatte found the Vietnamese and Lao people to be receptive in helping the U.S. task force and said most of the men he spoke to were his equivalent—former career military officers, not political appointees.

"We've been to every district, every village, multiple times. (We spoke to) people of all walks of life. They are delighted to be helpful," he said. "We don't want subterfuge. Former (NVA) officers have no reason to lie to us."

The NBC special, *Mystery on the Mountain*, aired in two parts in the summer of 1994. Kay Etchberger and her sons watched it together at Steve's home in Redlands, California, when they were gathered for Rich Etchberger's nearby wedding. Following the 1986 death of her father-in-law, Kay Etchberger moved back to her native Utah for a few years before going to live where Steve resided with his family, including the daughter, Traci, who was born the same day Dick Etchberger died. Steve remained in Southern California after separating from the Air Force in 1971 and had a long career as a United Parcel Service driver. The TV news special didn't mention Etchberger by name, but the family was glad to have a clearer understanding of the attack at Site 85. Kay Etchberger, 64, died of a heart attack due to complications of diabetes seven weeks after the NBC broadcasts and 26 1/2 years after her husband was killed in Laos.

Tim Castle called Rich Etchberger in October 1995 to say he was writing a book about Project Heavy Green and wanted some information about his father. Cory is the keeper of their father's records, so Rich asked him to help Castle, who told the brothers that their father's official Air Force history did not contain any evidence that he had earned the Air Force Cross, let alone been under consideration for the Medal of Honor. This surprised them since Cory had the medal, citation and even a picture of his mother accepting the decoration from McConnell, the Air Force chief of staff. Cory provided documentation to Castle, who forwarded it to Air Force personnel officials. They updated his father's records in 1998 to include mention of the Air Force Cross as recognition of his actions in Laos 30 years before. This move by the Air

Force and the subsequent publication of Castle's book, *One Day Too Long*, brought attention to the largely unknown Heavy Green mission and wider appreciation of Etchberger's actions. The Airman's Enlisted Heritage Hall at Maxwell-Gunter Air Force Base in Montgomery, Alabama, dedicated an exhibit in May 2000 that features a wax replica of the chief in a service-dress uniform donated by his family. The display also features details of his Site 85 actions and a movie of the mountain peak shot from a circling helicopter prior to the camp's construction. Etchberger's sons met Castle on this trip. At dinner together, he said he'd heard talk of Etchberger's Air Force Cross being upgraded to the Medal of Honor.

"We didn't think any more about this suggestion until a much later date," said Cory.

The same month as the Alabama dedication, the Air Force named a street for Etchberger at Tyndall Air Force Base near Panama City, Florida. In March 2006, Sheppard Air Force Base, Texas, dedicated Etchberger Hall, a $20 million, 300-room dormitory. Later that year, Lackland Air Force Base, Texas, where all Air Force enlistees attend boot camp, opened the Etchberger Training Complex. In 2008, a group of veterans dedicated a memorial at Barksdale Air Force Base, Louisiana, to men who served in the Combat Skyspot program during the Vietnam War. The memorial includes a tribute to Etchberger. In spring 2010, the Air Force Space Command presented the initial Etchberger Trophy to the top communications team in its Guardian Challenge competition at Peterson Air Force Base, Colorado. The ceremony was attended by Etchberger's sons and Site 85 battle survivor John Daniel.

By this time, a renewed move to recognize Etchberger with the Medal of Honor was well underway, and the impetus was from someone who never knew Etchberger. Retired Air Force Master Sgt. Robert L. Dilley of Bismarck, North Dakota, a participant in online military chat rooms, happened upon a discussion about Project Heavy Green. The Millville, Wisconsin, native had served in the military for 21 years as an auto track radar repairman. He joined the Air Force in 1973, five years after the attack on Phou Pha Thi, and served in various detachments of the 1st Combat Evaluation Group, Etchberger's old master unit. The more he read about the late chief's actions, the more he believed he should have received the Medal of Honor.

"I firmly believe that had he been on the east side of the border that night, there would have been no qualms with submitting him posthumously for it," he said.

In April 2004, Dilley drafted a letter to his congressman, Earl Pomeroy, requesting that he look into the actions of Etchberger for possible consideration of the Medal of Honor since the late GI had lived and worked in their state of North Dakota for six years. Dilley contacted Cory Etchberger to tell him what he was doing, then personally handed the letter to Pomeroy at an event honoring a National Guard unit. The next month, an aide to Pomeroy contacted Cory Etchberger for help in putting together a package for the congressman to present to the Air Force for review.

"It wasn't an easy process. We had to document actions of a 40-year-old illegal covert operation that occurred in a neutral country," said Cory, then a biology professor at Johnson County Community College in Overland Park, Kansas. "To proceed, we needed statements from two eye witnesses and by Jerry Clayton as commanding officer of the mission."

The men contacted Clayton, long retired from the service and living in Florida. He said he'd be happy to help them and mentioned that Etchberger had been considered for the Medal of Honor in 1968. In June 2004, Clayton contacted Sliz and Daniel and asked them to write letters detailing Dick's actions on that rock ledge 36 years earlier. The third man he'd helped rescue, William Husband, had since died. Sliz knew Etchberger well since they had been stationed together in North Dakota prior to being teamed for Project Heavy Green. The retired major wrote that "he was always the consummate NCO and deservedly rose through the ranks quickly. It came as no surprise that he was chosen for this highly sensitive assignment along with the other elite airmen. In spite of the fact that we had no combat training, when we were overrun, we managed to fight the enemy troops off repeatedly. (He) continuously fought back the enemy attacks. He managed to keep us from being wiped out by his tenacious defense of our position and, when the helicopter arrived, he assisted the wounded onto the jungle penetrator and into the aircraft." In his supporting document, Daniel said, "Dick never got hit and was directing me on what to do and what was taking place. He was able to get Stan and me loaded onto the chopper. I would not be alive were it not for Dick. He saved my life and the life of my comrades."

Clayton retrieved a copy of the earlier draft Medal of Honor recommendation from Frank Roura in California. The 1969 pledge of senior Air Force leaders to upgrade Etchberger's Air Force Cross hadn't been acted on in the ensuing 35 years. General James P. McConnell, the former Air Force chief of staff, died in 1986. Gen. John D. Ryan, his deputy, had assumed the role of chief of staff in August 1969 upon McConnell's retirement. Due to some health issues, it took Clayton a year to provide a supporting document to the package being prepared by Congressman Pomeroy's office, but the retired colonel had clear memories of interviewing Daniel and Sliz just days after the attack.

"Being the only one able to counter the enemies' actions, Sgt. Etchberger returned fire with his M-16 while his wounded crewmates passed ammunition to him. He held off the enemy until rescue helicopters arrived," the Project Heavy Green commander wrote. "At that time, he helped his wounded fellow crewmen into (a) sling so that they might be raised into the helicopter from the face of the cliff where they were trapped. After his crew and another survivor were safely aboard, Sgt. Etchberger finally got in the sling and was rescued. Without question, Sgt. Etchberger saved the lives of his operations officer and two other members of his crew."

In early 2005, a resident of Hamburg learned about Etchberger's actions through a display at the Air Force Sergeants Association's Airmen Memorial Museum in Suitland, Maryland. He contacted the *Reading Eagle* newspaper in Reading, Pennsylvania, which dispatched reporter Dan Kelly to track down the details of the Hamburg native's story. The newsman interviewed Etchberger's friends, his brother and other relatives, culminating with the February 13, 2005, publication of a front-page story under the headline, "Unheralded hero," which described the airmen's virtually unknown actions.

"One of America's bravest military heroes lies buried, unheralded, beneath a modest headstone on a windswept plot in St. John's Cemetery in Hamburg," Kelly's report began. It went on to note that the Air Force had honored the Pennsylvania native by naming streets and buildings after him and by erecting museum exhibits, "but there is no Etchberger Avenue in Hamburg or Etchberger

Hall at Hamburg High School, where he was the 1951 class president." The article prompted residents of his hometown to dedicate a plaque to the borough's native son on Memorial Day 2005, while his survivors participated that day in a parade and a ceremony honoring him. The *Reading Eagle* ran a follow-up front page article, "Unheralded no more."

Etchberger's story reached a larger audience when the Associated Press distributed Kelly's articles. The actions by the newspaper and Hamburg's citizenry prompted the area's congressional representative, Tim Holden, to join North Dakota's Pomeroy in support of the medal upgrade. They quickly introduced House Resolution 2674 to waive existing time limitations to allow the Medal of Honor to be awarded to Etchberger. It was just a procedural step allowing the president to present it, as the normal nomination for a medal must take place within two years of the date of the action, while it must be awarded within a year of that recommendation. Holden and Pomeroy had simply introduced the measure. Getting it into a legislative package for a vote was still several years away. The nudge given by North Dakota railroad worker Bob Dilley via a letter to a legislator had put this into motion. Dilley met Cory Etchberger at a 1st Combat Evaluation Group reunion in August 2005. By the next month, the file prepared by Pomeroy and his staff was ready to be submitted for review by Air Force personnel officials, who would see if Dick Etchberger met the criteria for consideration of the Medal of Honor while the legislative side did its work. Cory Etchberger was quietly hopeful but rued not having proof that a former Air Force chief of staff had agreed to push for a medal upgrade at a time when it wouldn't embarrass the country.

On December 8, 2005, the Department of Defense POW/Missing Personnel Office announced via a press release that remains of Tech. Sgt. Patrick L. Shannon, 33, a Project Heavy Green participant from Owasso, Oklahoma, had been identified after being found along the cliff at Phou Pha Thi and would be returned to his family for burial with full military honors:

> *The Joint POW/MIA Accounting Command began interviewing witnesses in both Laos and Vietnam in 1994 to gather information on the fates of the Americans who served at Mount*

Phou Pha Thi in March 1968. Some of those interviewed were villagers who lived near the site, while others were former enemy soldiers who carried out the attack. In 2002, one of the enemy soldiers stated that he helped throw the bodies of the Americans off the mountain after the attack, as they were unable to bury them on the rocky surface. Between 1994 and 2004, 11 investigations were conducted by both JPAC as well as unilaterally by Lao and Vietnamese investigators on both sides of the border. During one of the investigations, several mountaineer-qualified JPAC specialists scaled down the cliffs where they recovered remains and personal gear on ledges. JPAC and Armed Forces DNA Identification Laboratory scientists used mitochondrial DNA and other forensic techniques to identify the remains as those of Shannon.

His remains were buried April 15, 2006, at a service attended by 700 in Oklahoma City.

The Air Force Association, an independent, nonprofit, civilian organization that promotes public understanding of aerospace power and national defense, published an article on the fall of Site 85 in the April 2006 issue of its *Air Force* magazine. Cory Etchberger read the piece and sent a letter to the editor saying that his father was being considered for the Medal of Honor. It was published in the next issue and read by an 82-year-old retired colonel in Mississippi named Ruffin W. Gray. He, in turn, sent a letter to Cory Etchberger that filled in the last missing piece of evidence for his father to have the best chance at receiving the Medal of Honor. Gray had served as executive officer to Gen. John D. Ryan, the Air Force vice chief of staff when Etchberger received the Air Force Cross. Ryan was the final authority for approval of award of the service's eight highest medals. Ryan also had previous knowledge of Project Heavy Green as he had been commander of Pacific Air Forces at Hickam Air Force Base, Hawaii, in 1967-68 prior to assuming his Pentagon duties. Gray said Ryan directed him to review all of the recommendations regarding Etchberger's actions in Laos and give him his opinion on whether they met the criteria for the Medal of Honor. He did so and told the general they "met every element." Ryan reviewed the documents and concurred.

"However, due to the location of Lima Site 85, the conditions and circumstances under which they operated, and similar factors, the (United States) could not acknowledge or publicize this information," Gray's letter explained 37½ years later. "(Ryan) said that, while the Air Force Cross could be awarded without national media attention, there would be widespread publicity for the award of the (Medal of Honor)."

Gray suggested to his boss that Etchberger's records be flagged for annual review so the Air Force could award him the Medal of Honor when the United States could safely acknowledge what had transpired in Laos. Ryan agreed, and Gray assumed those steps would be carried out after his departure from the Pentagon. He told Cory Etchberger that he had thought of this plan over the years, wondering if anything had ever come of it. Gray told Cory Etchberger that he hoped Congress would pass House Resolution 2674 to allow the president to award the medal "and this is finally resolved the way it should be."

Cory Etchberger, now living with his wife and daughter in Switzerland, immediately understood the significance of Gray's letter. In fact, he believed it to be the most noteworthy piece of information supporting an upgrade of the medal as it confirmed Jerry Clayton's details of his 1968 discussion with General McConnell and provided firsthand knowledge of the circumstances surrounding the awarding of the Air Force Cross. Rep. Tim Holden sent a notarized statement from Gray to the Pentagon for inclusion in the medal consideration package being reviewed by an Air Force personnel panel.

In August 2008, Dick Etchberger's childhood pals June Kline and Don Yocom visited his grave and found a laminated letter from Ed Perrigo, who had served with their mutual friend in the Philippines 1965-67. He had driven from his home in Washington state earlier that year for an East Coast tour that included a stop at his late friend's Pennsylvania hometown followed by a visit to the Etchberger display at the Air Force enlisted museum in Montgomery, Alabama. Kline forwarded a copy of the letter to Cory Etchberger, who wrote to Perrigo. That fall, the retired senior master sergeant sent copies of three letters to Cory: two his father had written him from Thailand while working on Project Heavy Green and one from Kay Etchberger telling Perrigo that her husband had been killed.

"I firmly believe that if he had lived, he would have gone on to greater things, perhaps even chief master sergeant of the Air Force (the service's top enlisted spot). As it was to you and your family, Etch's untimely death was a shock to me and, like you, I miss him even today," Perrigo wrote to his friend's son.

In October 2008, following an internal review of documents describing Etchberger's actions during the attack of Lima Site 85, Secretary of the Air Force Michael Donley, the service's top civilian, nominated the Hamburg, Pennsylvania, native for the U.S. military's highest decoration, which is awarded "for conspicuous gallantry and intrepidity at the risk of life above and beyond the call of duty." The nomination was supported by Secretary of Defense Robert M. Gates and forwarded to President George W. Bush. At the same time, Donley wrote to the chairmen and ranking members of the Senate and House Armed Services Committees about Pomeroy and Holden's proposed legislation, asking for their help in giving special consideration for Etchberger since the normal timeline had long since expired. Law allows members of Congress to request reviews by a service secretary in such cases.

"This brave Airman clearly distinguished himself through his courageous actions," Donley wrote. "The Air Force and our nation are forever grateful for his heroic service."

Ultimately, Congressmen Pomeroy and Holden were able to include a clause authorizing such a waiver in the 2009 Duncan Hunter National Defense Authorization Act. President Bush signed the legislation, which included wording that the president "is authorized and requested to award the Medal of Honor" for Dick Etchberger's March 1968 actions. Still, this didn't mean Bush had actually approved the decoration, just that he could. This was very late in his second term though, and he didn't act on it, so the matter fell to Barack Obama when he was sworn in as president in January 2009. There was no word on the recommendation for more than a year, which frustrated Bob Dilley, who had purchased several dozen baseball caps featuring a design honoring Etchberger's projected Medal of Honor.

"I thought, 'Man, this is a shoe-in,'" he said. "I tried to keep my ear to the ground as much as I could, hoping to hear something. I never heard nothing. I was like, 'Damn.' Everything just pretty much went dead."

In May 2010, Cory Etchberger, now living and teaching college just 45 miles from Hamburg in suburban Philadelphia, received an email from Denise Harris, chief of Air Force Awards and Policy Programs at the Air Force Personnel Center, Randolph Air Force Base, Texas, asking for his telephone number in case the service had any questions about the nomination package. She contacted him again July 6, saying that the Air Force needed to reach him during a 60-minute window of time the next afternoon. He gathered his papers and waited for the call. At 1:30 p.m. July 7, 2010, the house telephone rang. It wasn't the Air Force at all, but an assistant to President Obama, asking Cory to hold for a call from him. Cory silently mouthed "It's the president" to his wife, Karen, and daughter, Madison. The 15-year-old dashed to pick up a phone in another room. A few seconds later, Obama came on the line.

"He said, 'Cory, this is the president' and I said, 'Yes, I recognize your voice, Mr. President.' He told me he was proud of my dad's actions and that he was very happy to approve the Medal of Honor," Cory remembered. "He said based on the recommendations from (the Air Force and Defense secretaries), he was going to authorize the medal. He called Dad a true American hero, and then he thanked me for keeping his memory alive for all of this time. I told him how glad I was that this was finally going to happen, and that it was him who would make the presentation."

The president ended the call by saying he was looking forward to hosting the Etchberger family at a White House ceremony to present the medal and his staff would be in touch regarding the arrangements. It was finally going to happen.

Cory, Karen and Madison hugged and cried. Karen's sister joined in as she was visiting their Schwenksville, Pennsylvania, home at the time. Cory called his brothers, both of whom thought he was kidding when he said he had just spoken to the president. He then sent an email to Dilley, asking him for his phone number. Dilley, who earlier in the year had considered destroying his Etchberger Medal of Honor caps out of frustration, was puzzled by the request since they always emailed each other.

"I knew it either got approved or it got canned," Dilley said. "Then I didn't hear from Cory right away and thought that damn package got crapped on. Someone threw it in File 13. I was just sure of it. Finally, the phone rang, and it came up, 'Cory Etchberger.' I said, 'Hello, Cory' and he said, 'Bob, get out the box of hats' and I said, 'No shit?' I was ecstatic. Tears in the eyes. I was on an emotional high for about a week. I couldn't believe it."

A White House staff member asked Cory to coordinate with family members to find a suitable date for the ceremony that would fit into the president's schedule. The staffer also asked Cory to not go to the news media until the White House could announce the Medal of Honor decision with a firm presentation date. In late summer, the White House decided the medal would be presented Tuesday, September 21, 2010. Etchberger family members and friends gathered in Washington, D.C., a few days before the ceremony. Among those who attended was retired Technical Sgt. John Daniel, one of the surviving men who Etchberger had protected overnight and helped rescue. The other, Maj. Stan Sliz, was unable to attend, as was retired Col. Jerry Clayton, the Project Heavy Green commander, both for health reasons. Also present were pilot Ken Wood and crew chief Rusty Irons, the helicopter crewmen who plucked Etchberger and three others off Phou Pha Thi in 1968, and retired Col. Joe Panza, a pilot on the helicopter crew that, with pararescuemen, subsequently rescued Staff Sgt. Jack Starling from the peak. Dilley traveled from North Dakota wearing a jacket featuring a 1st Combat Evaluation Group patch and toting his collection of caps to distribute.

The day before the White House ceremony, Etchberger's sons visited CIA headquarters at the invitation of Dr. Tim Castle, the *One Day Too Long* author who worked at the Langley, Virginia, campus. He had arranged for them to meet Michael Morrell, the CIA deputy director, but upon their arrival he instead led them to the office of its director, Leon Panetta. The next day, the brothers were joined by their extended family members in an Oval Office visit with President Obama and First Lady Michelle Obama. The family gave the couple a signed copy of Castle's book. It was soon time for a ceremony 42½ years in the making. Sitting in the front row, to the president's left as he spoke, were several Medal of Honor recipients, recognizable due to the decorations hanging from their necks by powder blue ribbons. At the behest of Etchberger's survivors, the president's remarks mentioned the actions of Dilley, who spurred on the discussion of a Medal of Honor for an airman he'd never met—one who had been killed, in fact, while Dilley was a junior high school student. He was stunned to hear the president utter his name.

"I was in awe and had goosebumps. I'm just a little ol' country boy from Millville, Wisconsin. When I got to the White House, I thought 'I don't believe this is happening' and the notoriety I experienced after the ceremony was something. Several generals came up to me to thank me."

Etchberger's son, Richard, accepted the medal from the president while accompanied by his brothers. Steve Wilson, the normally stoic stepson who has the clearest memories of Etchberger among the three brothers, wept openly.

An Air Force recipient of the Medal of Honor is uncommon. Of the 3,469 decorations presented going back to the Civil War, only 60 were to airmen, including those who flew in World War II before the Air Force became a separate service from the Army. It's even rarer for an enlisted airman to earn it. Etchberger is just the seventh Air Force enlisted man to receive the medal. Most of those honored with the decoration have been pilots and, therefore, commissioned officers. Etchberger was the 13th airman, whether enlisted or officer, recognized for actions in the Vietnam War. Etchberger, who would have been 77 at the time of the White House ceremony, is only the third enlisted Air Force Medal of Honor recipient from the Vietnam War. For more than 30 years there was only one: Airman 1st Class John Levitow, 23, an AC-47 gunship loadmaster cited for his actions during a February 24, 1969, mission when his aircraft was hit by a mortar round. Though suffering from more than 40 shrapnel wounds, he threw himself on a smoking magnesium flare, dragging it under him to an open cargo door. It ignited just as he had pushed it from the aircraft. Levitow survived his injuries and was a frequent presence at military events until his death, from cancer, at age 55 on Nov. 8, 2000.

Just a month later, an Air Force Cross presented posthumously in 1966 to Airman 1st Class William Pitsenbarger, 21, was upgraded to the Medal of Honor. The pararescueman was aboard an HH-43 Huskie helicopter sent to evacuate wounded soldiers from the 1st Infantry Division who were surrounded by a Vietcong battalion in the jungle near Saigon. He volunteered to be lowered from a hovering chopper with a rifle and medical bag. His work enabled his aircraft and another Huskie crew to evacuate nine soldiers, while he remained behind to aid more wounded. The firefight grew so intense that the helicopters could not return. Pitsenbarger collected and distributed ammunition to the surviving soldiers until he was mortally wounded.

Etchberger is the lone Air Force senior NCO to receive the Medal of Honor and the highest-ranking enlisted GI from any service branch to have earned it.

Medal of Honor Criteria

The Medal of Honor is awarded by the president in the name of Congress to a person who, while a member of the armed forces, distinguishes himself or herself conspicuously by gallantry and intrepidity at the risk of his life or her life above and beyond the call of duty while engaged in an action against an enemy of the United States; while engaged in military operations involving conflict with an opposing foreign force; or while serving with friendly foreign forces engaged in an armed conflict against an opposing armed force in which the United States is not a belligerent party. The deed performed must have been one of personal bravery or self-sacrifice so conspicuous as to clearly distinguish the individual above his or her comrades and must have involved risk of life. Incontestable proof of the performance of service is exacted, and each recommendation for award of this decoration is considered on the standard of extraordinary merit.

Remarks by President Obama

Sept. 21, 2010, prior to presentation of Medal of Honor

Of all the military decorations that our nation can bestow, the highest is the Medal of Honor. It is awarded for conspicuous gallantry; for risking one's life in action; for serving above and beyond the call of duty. Today, we present the Medal of Honor to an American who displayed such gallantry more than four decades ago—Chief Master Sergeant Richard L. Etchberger.

This medal reflects the gratitude of an entire nation. So we are also joined by Vice President Biden and members of Congress, including Congressman Earl Pomeroy and—from Chief Etchberger's home state of Pennsylvania—Congressman Tim Holden.

We are joined by leaders from across my administration, including Secretary of Veterans Affairs Ric Shinseki; Secretary of Defense Robert Gates; Vice Chairman of the Joint Chiefs of Staff General Jim "Hoss" Cartwright; and leaders from across our armed services, including Air Force Secretary Michael Donley and Chief of Staff General Norton Schwartz.

I want to acknowledge a group of Americans who understand the valor we recognize today, because they displayed it themselves—members of the Medal of Honor Society. Most of all, we welcome Dick Etchberger's friends and family—especially his brother Robert, and Dick's three sons, Steve, Richard and Cory.

For the Etchberger family, this is a day more than 40 years in the making. Cory was just nine years old, but he can still remember that winter in 1969 when he, his brothers and his mom were escorted to the Pentagon. The war in Vietnam was still raging. Dick Etchberger had given his life a year earlier. Now his family was being welcomed by the Air Force chief of staff.

In a small, private ceremony, Dick was recognized with the highest honor that the Air Force can give—the Air Force Cross. These three sons were told that their dad was a hero—that he had died while saving his fellow airmen. But they weren't told much else. Their father's work was classified, and for years, that's all they really knew.

Then, nearly two decades later, the phone rang. It was the Air Force, and their father's mission was finally being declassified. And that's when they learned the truth—that their father had given his life not in Vietnam, but in neighboring Laos. That's when they began to learn the true measure of their father's heroism.

Dick Etchberger was a radar technician and he had been handpicked for a secret assignment. With a small team of men, he served at the summit of one of the tallest mountains in Laos—more than a mile high, literally above the clouds. They manned a tiny radar station, guiding American pilots in the air campaign against North Vietnam.

Dick and his crew believed they could help turn the tide of the war, perhaps even end it. And that's why North Vietnamese forces were determined to shut it down. They sent their planes to strafe the Americans as they worked. They moved in their troops. And eventually, Dick and his team could look through their binoculars and see that their mountain was surrounded by thousands of North Vietnamese troops.

Dick and his crew at that point had a decision to make—ask to be evacuated or continue the mission for another day. They believed that no one could possibly scale the mountain's steep cliffs. And they believed in their work. So they stayed. They continued their mission.

There were 19 Americans on the mountain that evening. When their shift was over, Dick and his four men moved down to a small, rocky ledge on a safer side of the mountain. And then, during the night, the enemy attacked. Somehow, fighters scaled the cliffs and overran the summit. Down the side of the mountain, Dick and his men were now trapped on that ledge.

The enemy lobbed down grenade after grenade, hour after hour. Dick and his men would grab those grenades and throw them back, or kick them into the valley below. But the grenades kept coming. One

136

airman was killed, and then another. A third airman was wounded, and then another. Eventually, Dick was the only man standing.

As a technician, he had no formal combat training. In fact, he had only recently been issued a rifle. But Dick Etchberger was the very definition of an NCO—a leader determined to take care of his men. When the enemy started moving down the rocks, Dick fought them off. When it looked like the ledge would be overrun, he called for air strikes, within yards of his own position, shaking the mountain and clearing the way for a rescue. And in the morning light, an American helicopter came into view.

Richard Etchberger lived the Airman's Creed—to never leave an airman behind, to never falter, to never fail. So as the helicopter hovered above and lowered its sling, Dick loaded his wounded men, one by one, each time exposing himself to enemy fire. And when another airman suddenly rushed forward after eluding the enemy all night, Dick loaded him, too—and finally, himself. They had made it off the mountain.

That's when it happened. The helicopter began to peel away. A burst of gunfire erupted below. Dick was wounded. And by the time they landed at the nearest base, he was gone.

Of those 19 men on the mountain that night, only seven made it out alive. Three of them owed their lives to the actions of Dick Etchberger. Today, we're honored to be joined by one of them—Mr. John Daniel.

Among the few who knew of Dick's actions, there was a belief that his valor warranted our nation's highest military honor. But his mission had been a secret. And that's how it stayed for those many years. When their father's mission was finally declassified, these three sons learned something else. It turned out that their mother had known about Dick's work all along. But she had been sworn to secrecy. And she kept that promise—to her husband and her country—all those years, not even telling her own sons. So today is also a tribute to Catherine Etchberger, and a reminder of the extraordinary sacrifices that our military spouses make on behalf of our nation.

This story might have ended there—with a family finally knowing the truth. And for another two decades, it did. But today also marks another chapter in a larger story of our nation finally honoring that generation of Vietnam veterans who served with dedication and courage but all too often were shunned when they came home, which was a disgrace that must never happen again.

A few years ago, an airman who never even knew Dick Etchberger read about his heroism and felt he deserved something more. So he wrote his congressman, who made it his mission to get this done. Today we thank that airman, retired Master Sergeant Robert Dilley, and that congressman, Earl Pomeroy, who along with Congressman Holden made this day possible.

Sadly, Dick's wife Catherine did not live to see this moment. But today Steve and Richard and Cory—today your nation finally acknowledges and fully honors your father's bravery. Because even though it has been 42 years, it's never too late to do the right thing. And it's never too late to pay tribute to our Vietnam veterans—and their families.

In recent years, Dick's story has become known and Air Force bases have honored him with streets and buildings in his name. And at the base where he trained so long ago in Barksdale—Barksdale in Louisiana, there is a granite monument with an empty space next to his name—and that space can finally be etched with the words "Medal of Honor."

But the greatest memorial of all to Dick Etchberger is the spirit that we feel here today, the love that inspired him to serve—love for his country and love for his family. And most eloquent—the most eloquent expression of that devotion are the words that he wrote himself, to a friend back home just months before he gave his life to our nation.

"I hate to be away from home," he wrote from that small base above the clouds, "but I believe in the job." He said, "It is the most challenging job I'll ever have in my life." And then he added, "I love it."

Our nation endures because there are patriots like Chief Master Sergeant Richard Etchberger—and our troops who are serving as we speak—who love this nation and defend it. Their legacy lives on because their families and fellow citizens preserve it. And as Americans, we remain worthy of their example only so long as we honor it—not merely with the medals that we present, but by remaining true to the values and freedoms for which they fight.

Milan

- pass out notices
- read book ≈9:30/9:35
- file leveled books + take to Bookroom

Citation Accompanying Awarding of the Medal of Honor to Air Force Chief Master Sgt. Richard L. Etchberger

The President of the United States of America, authorized by Act of Congress, March 3, 1863, has awarded, in the name of the Congress, the Medal of Honor to Chief Master Sergeant Richard L. Etchberger, United States Air Force, for conspicuous gallantry and intrepidity at the risk of life above and beyond the call of duty.

Chief Master Sergeant Richard L. Etchberger distinguished himself by extraordinary heroism on March 11, 1968, in the country of Laos, while assigned as a ground radar superintendent, Detachment 1, 1043rd Radar Evaluation Squadron.

On that day, Chief Etchberger and his team of technicians were manning a top-secret defensive position at Lima Site 85 when the base was overrun by an enemy ground force. Receiving sustained and withering heavy artillery attacks directly upon his unit's position, Chief Etchberger's entire crew lay dead or severely wounded. Despite having received little or no combat training, Chief Etchberger single-handedly held off the enemy with an M-16, while simultaneously directing air strikes into the area and calling for air rescue. Because of his fierce defense and heroic and selfless actions, he was able to deny the enemy access to his position and save the lives of his remaining crew. With the arrival of the rescue aircraft, Chief Etchberger, without hesitation, repeatedly and deliberately risked his own life, exposing himself to heavy enemy fire in order to place three surviving wounded comrades into rescue slings hanging from the hovering helicopter waiting to airlift them to safety. With his remaining crew safely aboard, Chief Etchberger finally climbed into an evacuation sling himself, only to be fatally wounded by enemy ground fire as he was being raised into the aircraft.*

Chief Etchberger's bravery and determination in the face of persistent enemy fire and overwhelming odds are in keeping with the highest standards of performance and traditions of military service. Chief Etchberger's gallantry, self-sacrifice and profound concern for his fellow men at risk of his life, above and beyond the call of duty, reflect the highest credit upon himself and the United States Air Force.

---

* Etchberger was killed by a bullet that passed through the fuselage of the helicopter after he had safely reached it, not as he was being raised on the hoist.

Afterword

by Cory Etchberger

I haven't eaten strawberry shortcake since the night of March 12, 1968. My mom served the dessert to me and my brother, Rich, just before taking a phone call saying that my father had been killed in Southeast Asia. Besides the shock, pain and anguish I immediately felt, I knew my life would be changed forever now that my dad was dead. I was just 9, a year younger than Rich.

As a small child, I thought if I could just forget everything about that day, maybe it hadn't really happened. Now in my 50s, I've spent the last few years trying to remember everything I can about my father.

A few days after Dad's body arrived in Hamburg, the funeral parlor downtown set up a viewing. In our home, my mother was getting dressed in a dark gray dress. Rich was putting on a sport coat and tie. My dad's parents arrived to take us to the mortuary. I was in my room and hadn't put on any dress clothes. Mom came upstairs to ask why, and I said I didn't want to go. I was scared. I had never seen a dead person before.

What I didn't tell her was that I thought my father was going to be bloody and displayed in a black, Dracula-like coffin standing in a corner. I steadfastly refused to go and, eventually, my mom had a neighbor come to the house to stay with me while the rest of the family went to the service.

The next day, my grandfather took me into Hamburg to Miller's 5 & 10, which he had run for more than 20 years. After we had been in the store for an hour or so, he took me by the hand and very gently said, "Come on. Let's go see your father."

The funeral home was right across the street from his shop. We walked into it, and I saw a silver pewter casket with an open lid. The inside was covered with a puffy white satin material. I approached it, peered in and saw my father under a glass window. He was wearing a dress blue Air Force uniform. His hands were crossed and had white gloves on them. His hair was just like he usually combed it, and I noticed he was wearing a bit of makeup. Other than that, it looked just like him. There was no blood, of course, and I wasn't scared at all.

I didn't really know much, if anything, about the true nature of his death at that point. I just knew my dad wasn't coming back to us. The next winter, we were whisked to the Pentagon for a ceremony in which my father received the Air Force Cross. I didn't understand the significance of the day. My oldest brother, Steve, came from California where he served in the Air Force as a C-141 Starlifter transport mechanic. He'd been working on the flightline one day when he was summoned to report to the office of the commander of the 63rd Military Airlift Wing. He wondered what he'd done to be called by the top officer in his unit. The colonel told him to get his dress blue uniform ready and to shave his mustache because he was going to the Pentagon.

I remember the ceremony as being quite somber. Someone read the medal citation that said he'd saved some lives. It was all just white noise to the young me. Many people asked me over the years if I thought it was strange that Dad was awarded the high-level decoration for dying in a helicopter crash. I was 9, so what did I know? I thought everyone who died in a chopper accident got one. For years I didn't grasp that the Air Force Cross is an extremely high recognition for valor, second only to the Medal of Honor. At the time my dad received it, he was only the 19th enlisted airman to earn it dating back to Word War II.

Mom continued to keep secret what she fully knew about Dad's passing until her own death in 1994. She signed secrecy agreements at the Pentagon in 1967, and she promised my dad she would not reveal anything until she was told she was allowed to do so. Nobody ever told her she could, so she didn't. From 1969 to 1994, Mom kept Dad's paperwork, Air Force Cross citation and the medal itself in a box at the very back of her bedroom closet. She never displayed any military memorabilia or even put out many pictures of him around the house.

In retrospect, I think that was one way for her to keep that promise she made to her husband. If the Air Force Cross was out for visitors to see, it would have led to unwanted questions from family and friends.

I remember talking directly to my Mom about Dad only three times. The first was when I was a junior in high school. A teacher of mine was teaching us about various forms of government. I went home and told Mom that we had learned about communism. She said, "You know, your father died fighting communism."

The second time we talked about him was in 1978 on the 10th anniversary of his death. I was in college, and she called to remind me that he'd been gone a decade. I told her I'd already remembered.

The third instance was in January 1994, two weeks after I turned 35, when I called my mother to chat with her in California. Just before she hung up, she mentioned that I had now lived longer than my father, who died six days after his 35th birthday.

It may sound strange that we did not talk about him all that much while I was growing up in Hamburg. Mom was busy raising Rich and me. Steve was in California starting a family of his own. My grandparents helped Mom as much as they could. Now that I'm a father, I can only imagine the anguish they suffered because of their son's death.

When a child loses a parent, you don't have a lot of your own memories of them. What you have is stories told to you by people; in my case, it was those of my older brothers and friends of my father from his military career and even back to his childhood. In a way, their memories have become my own, and I am beyond grateful for them.

In retrospect, I wish now that I had asked many more questions of my mom and grandparents as all three of them took things to their grave I wish I knew about my father. How remarkable if they could have been at the Medal of Honor ceremony at the White House to see a U.S. president speak glowingly about Dad's character and his actions atop a foreign peak long ago in the service of our country.

The trip to the White House for the ceremony was a proud time for the Etchbergers. Each of the 15 family members wore watches on our right wrists with the face of the watch pointing inward just like Dad used to wear his. I brought the Timex he was wearing when he was killed and kept it in my suit coat pocket along with a picture of him.

We received a private White House tour prior to the ceremony and were then asked to step into the Roosevelt Room prior to meeting President Obama and First Lady Michelle Obama in the Oval Office. They were both very gracious and said they wanted us to be at ease and that it was going to be a great ceremony to honor Dad. We presented the president with a signed copy of Dr. Tim Castle's book, *One Day Too Long*, and a Medal of Honor coin we had designed featuring Dad's likeness. The ceremony was a fitting tribute to both Dad and all of the brave airmen who served atop Phou Pha Thi.

After the ceremony, the family was part of a receiving line in the Blue Room to welcome guests before a lunch was served in the State Dining Room. The White House staff must have heard us talk about how much our family adores dogs because suddenly we were ushered into a private room to meet the "first dog," Bo. We then were led out to the South Lawn for pictures taken in front of the White House's South Portico.

Many people have asked me what my father would have to say about receiving the Medal of Honor. I know his response would have been, "I wish I could have saved more lives." He would also want for the men who served with at him Site 85 not to be forgotten. Partial remains of Tech Sgt. Pat Shannon, 33, were returned to his family in 2006. On Sept. 15, 2012, two years after the White House Medal of Honor ceremony, the partial remains of Lt. Col. Bill Blanton, 46, were buried in his hometown of El Reno, Oklahoma. They, too, were found along the cliff at Phou Pha Thi. Nine other families have not been able to bury their loved ones, however. Ours is fortunate in that we were the only one to have a body to bury in the aftermath of the battle of Site 85.

Even though we had invited Maj. Stan Sliz to attend the Medal of Honor ceremony, his poor health precluded him from joining us. He suffered from ailments related to his 1968 injuries for the remainder of his life. A few weeks after the ceremony, I called Stan to chat with him about our experience and to see how he was doing. He knew my father quite well because they had worked together in Bismarck, North Dakota, for several years in the early 1960s, well before each was chosen for Project Heavy Green. We talked and cried together on the phone for an hour. He said he was still haunted by what happened on the mountain that night and still had a very difficult time dealing with my father's death. Stan is haunted no more. He died in March 2013, just months after doing an in-person interview for this book.

Col. Jerry Clayton could not attend the ceremony either. He agonized over the loss of his men for decades. I called him to thank him for all of his efforts over the years to recognize my father's actions and to provide some closure to the families of his men. Jerry thought the world of Dad. Our phone call was so tearful that each of us had to pause to let the other regain his composure. Jerry finished the conversation with a lovely assessment of Dad.

"His interest in his people was a talent he exhibited constantly. His people loved him and would do anything for him," said Jerry, who passed away in August 2013. "His final moments gave a striking example of how he took care of his men."

After the excitement of the Medal of Honor ceremony and a subsequent service in which Dad was inducted into the Pentagon's Hall of Heroes faded, we began to think about how we could continue Dad's legacy of caring for others. Ultimately, we asked ourselves, "What good can come from his death, even after 40 years?" As a result, we formed a non-profit foundation in his name with the purpose of helping others. We provide leadership awards, scholarships, help Air Force families and share the story of the men of Project Heavy Green.

The Air Force continues to recognize my father in many ways. It has dedicated streets, buildings and dormitories to him and has added his name to a number of monuments on Air Force bases around the world. Steve, Rich and I are often invited to attend dedication ceremonies, at which we are always warmly welcomed back into the Air Force family. It means so much to us that Dad is being fully recognized now. His story was, at first, kept secret out of necessity and, later, simply untold even in his own service.

While at these bases, I share some personal experiences about Dad with airmen, who often ask if we're bitter that it took so long for our father to receive the Medal of Honor. The answer is a resounding, "No!" Of course, I wish my mother had lived to accept his Medal of Honor, just as she accepted his Air Force Cross in 1969, but I don't dwell on what I wish would have happened in the past. I can only continue to share his story and pass on his legacy of helping to future generations.

Epilogue

Willliam H. Sullivan

William H. Sullivan served as ambassador to Laos until March 1969 and was succeeded by Nixon-appointee George McMurtrie Godley that summer. Sullivan spent much of the early 1970s as the deputy assistant secretary of state for East Asian and Pacific affairs, working closely with future Secretary of State Henry Kissinger, then the national security adviser, in lengthy war negotiations in Paris with North Vietnam representatives. Sullivan served as ambassador to the Philippines 1973–1977 and subsequently in the same post in Iran until spring 1979. He left the country about six months before 52 U.S. Embassy staffers were taken hostage. He soon retired from government service and died Oct. 11, 2013, in Washington, D.C., at age 90.

Souvanna Phouma

Souvanna Phouma continued as prime minister of Laos until communists took control in 1975 and established the People's Democratic Republic of Laos, ending six centuries of monarchic rule. The government aligned itself with Vietnam and the Soviet bloc. Souvanna Phouma died in January 1984 at age 82 in Vientiane, where he had remained after losing power. The United States resumed full diplomatic relations with Laos in 1992 following the collapse of the Soviet Union.

Jerry Clayton

Col. Jerry Clayton, the Heavy Green commander, suffered from the loss of his men for the rest of his life, which ended at age 89 in September 2013.

"I went through some rough times for awhile," he said. "I've searched and searched and searched there in my mind, and I've worn out a couple of shrinks. I've come to understand now that there wasn't a real hell of a lot I could do about it."

He and Lt. Col. Bill Blanton, onsite at Phou Pha Thi March 10, 1968, agreed on a course of action, though neither knew that as they did enemy soldiers were scaling the cliff below the radar camp.

"About 10 p.m., I was told that things had turned . . . that they were getting more rocket fire. So I got on a teletype conference and in the end I told Bill, 'You're up there and I'm here and I can't tell you, I won't tell you, what to do. You do what you think is best.'

"I'm still sick about that. I don't know what I could have done had I told him to get out of there 'cause he knew I didn't have the authority, and until the ambassador launched the search force, the rescue force, there was no way out of that place anyway except down that trail, and the enemy was there. The last words that came out of there came (via teletype) from Mel Holland, who closed saying, 'See you later, I hope.' That's the way (it) happened. I bear as much blame, probably, as the ambassador."

The next thing Clayton heard was from CIA sources telling him that the site had been overrun.

"To my dying day, I will wish I had been there, but I was not and I can't do anything about it now. People thought I sat on my ass at Udorn."

Clayton initially kept a lot of items related to the attack but eventually threw most of it away, including the bullet that was removed from Etchberger's body.

"Looking back on it now, I don't know if it would mean anything to (the family) or not. It's kind of a gory thing, actually," said Clayton, who was immediately impressed with Etchberger upon meeting him in 1954 in Sacramento, California, when the young airman came from Utah to attend UHF radio school near Clayton's radar bomb scoring detachment. "In the end, I caused his death by sending for him when I needed him."

Stan Sliz

Maj. Stan Sliz had health complications the rest of his days from wounds he suffered in the Site 85 attack. He had septic shock, lost toes and part of a foot, and shrapnel remained in his body. He suffered two heart attacks, including a fatal one in March 2013 at age 80. The fall before his death, he acknowledged that nightmares were still a problem for him. His wife, Ann, is proud of how he rebounded from the trauma.

"He's a model for our kids, for him to go through that and survive and flourish," she said.

After his reassignment to Hickam Air Force Base on Oahu the summer after the attack, he was the assistant base operations officer and helped plan the fall 1968 Waikiki Beach visit by the Thunderbirds, the official Air Force aerial demonstration team. A navigator prior to becoming a radar controller, he eventually returned to flying status on C-118 Liftmasters, participating in courier flights to the Far East, bringing inspector general teams to their destinations and shuttling legislators around the Pacific.

Later, when not flying, he worked at the Hickam command post. He answered the phone there one day in 1970 and found himself on the line with a newspaper reporter saying he wanted to talk to him about his time in Laos. Sliz hung up on him. He soon found himself giving a deposition, though, to a legislative committee looking into U.S. operations in Laos.

The Slizes had warm memories of Kay Etchberger, Dick's widow, from their time living near each other in North Dakota in the early 1960s. The Etchbergers' oldest son, Steve, even babysat the Sliz children in Bismarck. Kay later visited the couple in Hawaii.

"She was grieving, but she was OK," said Ann Sliz. "She was a pretty strong lady."

Stan's injuries jolted Ann into action. She was a science teacher in Bismarck when he was hurt, and she realized the family couldn't survive on her salary alone in case Stan died from his injuries or was medically retired from the service. She went back to school at the University of Hawaii.

"I made a really interesting decision at that point. I thought, 'Well, this is a wakeup call.' If something happens to Stan and he doesn't make it, I've got to find a way to support these kids. So I was determined I was going to go out and get more education. That was my big turning point."

She recalls being taunted by students saying that her husband was a baby killer and remembers a few professors asking why she was taking up space in a program that a man could have filled. Undeterred, she earned a master's degree in zoology and a doctorate in anatomy. She did cancer research after Stan retired from the Air Force in December 1972. The family moved to Colorado, where Stan took a position in office machine sales as a manufacturer's representative, ran his own business in communications and eventually worked at a casino before he and Ann moved to Prescott, Arizona, and finally, to Huntington Beach, California, to live with their daughter, Lee, and her husband, Konrad Kern.

John Daniel

As his teammate Stan Sliz had before his death, Technical Sgt. John Daniel still suffers from nightmares and takes medications, including antidepressants related to his injuries and enduring the attack atop Phou Pha Thi.

"How you gonna keep from it? It's there," said Daniel, 76, who lives in La Junta, Colorado, where the Air Force first sent him in 1961.

He recuperated for more than a year before becoming an electronics instructor in 1969 at Keesler Air Force Base in Biloxi, Mississippi. He returned to La Junta and resumed radar-related duties in 1972 and soon completed a six-month radar assignment in Thailand. Daniel retired from the Air Force in 1979 after serving 20 years. He operated a bar before buying an account management company in 1984. He gave up the bookkeeping part around 2010 but still does tax preparation work. He had three children—Jerry, Jean and Jane—with his first wife, Josephine. Their marriage ended in divorce, and he married a second time in 1988. His wife, Sheryl, died in July 2014.

He never again saw in person anyone who endured the attack with him or visited with his former commander, Clayton, except by phone or email. He has seen administrative man Frank Roura and Donnell Hill, a radar technician who served on the crew that split Site 85 duties with that of Daniel's team.

Ken Wood

Air America helicopter pilot Ken Wood was 28 when he flew the rescue mission in March 1968, just 11 months after he left the Army following a tour of duty in Vietnam. He flew out of Thailand for six years before moving to Saigon in March 1973. He spent eight years with Air America before returning to the United States to attend Embry-Riddle Aeronautical University in Daytona Beach, Florida, and join the Florida National Guard as a UH-1 Huey pilot.

Wood transferred to a National Guard unit in Texas to fly CH-47 Chinook helicopters when he took a civilian position at General Dynamics' F-16 Fighting Falcon manufacturing plant in Fort Worth. He retired from the National Guard as a chief warrant officer 4 in 1989 with 20 years of military service. Wood was involved with other rescues in Southeast Asia but said the Site 85 one stands out because it involved more than one person.

"Usually, two ships would pick up two people or something like that," said Wood, 75, who lives in Houston. "(That) rescue is the most memorable. It really made me feel like I did something. I had a lot of satisfaction. What goes through my mind, had I backed off that a mountain a second earlier or five seconds later, maybe Etchberger might be around today. I don't know that, and I'll never know that."

He mentioned that to Etchberger's son, Cory, during the festivities surrounding the Medal of Honor presentation. Cory told him it was OK to let it go.

"What's ironic is that I flew a thousand hours with the Army in Vietnam and never took a hit," he said. "I flew with Air Amerca and (brought) an aircraft home that looked like Swiss cheese. The war had intensified."

Rusty Irons

Rusty Irons, the 28-year-old crew chief on the chopper that brought Sliz, Daniel and Husband to safety—and on which Etchberger was shot—worked for Air America until 1972. The mission didn't stand out much to him until he heard about the push to nominate Etchberger for a Medal of Honor.

"Now I think about it most of the time. One of the bad things about this is that it brings back memories," said Irons, 75. "In those days, you forgot it after a couple of days, you know, whatever, and went onto something else. Usually you remember the funny (absurd) things, but this was not a funny thing."

Irons recalls that Etchberger made it aboard the chopper before being shot and believes the fatal round passed through the wooden stock of Irons' AK-47 rifle before hitting Etchberger. Irons was sitting on a flak vest and had a toolbox under his seat for more protection when the burst of gunfire hit.

"You would try to make yourself as small as possible," said Irons, who roomed for a time in Thailand with Glen Woods, the Air America crew chief who shot down the biplanes that attacked Phou Pha Thi in January 1968. Woods later died in a chopper crash.

Irons got "the shakes" from anxiety and quit flying but remained in Southeast Asia, performing dual duties as assistant chief flight mechanic and head of the engine overhaul shop at the CIA site of Long Tieng, Laos. By 1972, he'd had enough of the war and returned to his native California. He worked in helicopter maintenance for the Los Angeles County Fire Department air operations' branch from 1972 to 2004, later continuing there as a consultant. He had more than 10,000 flying hours in Southeast Asia at a rate of 100 to 150 per month. He admits the total is a soft number.

"This is all a guess," the jovial Irons said during a January 2011 interview at his home in Southern California. "It depends on who I'm drinking with. One night I had four drinks, and I think it was up to 12,000."

He saw pilot Ken Wood for the first time in more than 40 years when both traveled to Washington, D.C., in 2010 to attend Etchberger's Medal of Honor ceremony.

Frank Roura

Then-Master Sgt. Frank Roura was the administrative senior NCO for Project Heavy Green's headquarters at Udorn Air Base. He was also Etchberger's roommate in an off-base rental home, but the mission wasn't his first time in Thailand or even his initial experience at being "sheep dipped" to conceal his identity as a serviceman. He had resigned from the Air Force to become a Lockheed Aircraft Services employee, at least on paper, for a 1965–1966 temporary duty assignment at Udorn.

Roura, 87, a native of Washington Heights in New York City, was later assigned to Arizona; the Pentagon; Castle Air Force Base, California; and Panama before taking his final Air Force job with the Office of Special Investigations at Travis Air Force Base northeast of San Francisco. He retired in 1977 as a chief master sergeant. His wife, Jeane, died in 1997, and he lived with his daughter, Sam, in Half Moon Bay, California, before moving into a longterm healthcare facility run by the Department of Veterans Affairs.

Joe Panza

Co-pilot to Capt. Russell L. Cayler on the HH-53 search and rescue chopper crew that was next at the peak after Wood and Irons, Capt. Joe Panza remained in the Air Force for 28 years, retiring as a colonel in 1992. Panza, who served for six years as a Navy enlisted man prior to receiving an officer's commission, is executive director of the Air University Foundation, supporting educational efforts of the Air Force professional military education system at Maxwell Air Force Base in Montgomery, Alabama.

He arrived at Udorn Air Base in August 1967, just before the Project Heavy Green men did. Panza later flew fixed-wing aircraft, including the C-9 Nightingale and C-141 Starlifter. During Operation Homecoming in 1973, he brought Vietnam War prisoners of war home following their release from the Hanoi Hilton prison camp.

Panza met Etchberger's sons and other family members when the Air Force dedicated an exhibit in the late chief master sergeant's honor in May 2000 at the Enlisted Heritage Hall at the Gunter Annex to Maxwell Air Force Base.

Hal Strack

Brig. Gen. Harold Arthur "Hal" Strack was commander of the 1st Radar Bombardment Scoring Group at Carswell Air Force Base in Fort Worth, Texas, when Etchberger was a sergeant in a subordinate outfit in Salt Lake City in the late 1950s. Strack, a pioneer in ground-directed radar bomb scoring, was an early admirer of the young NCO and personally chose him for an assignment to Morocco to work with two strong master sergeants.

"He just, to a great extent, inserted and asserted himself. He was not only the number one maintenance man and number one operations man, he was almost the first sergeant of the detachment," Strack said in 2010. "He was close to being—if not in fact, if not technically—one of the commanders, one of the people who ran the detachment."

Strack left the radar bomb scoring field and last saw Etchberger, then a senior master sergeant, around 1964 when the colonel was one of the top officers in the 90th Strategic Missile Wing at F.E. Warren Air Force Base, Wyoming. He wasn't surprised to see that the sergeant had been promoted twice in the previous five years.

"He just kept going like that. He was always, always thought that highly of. He was always put in key and important jobs," said Strack, who returned to the 90th Strategic Missile Wing as commander in 1969. He retired from the Air Force in 1974 as a brigadier general after serving as chief of a division of the Joint Chiefs of Staff. He lived in Incline Village, Nevada, for nearly a quarter-century before his death in 2014.

Strack didn't learn of Etchberger's death, or the circumstances surrounding it, until long after it happened when he heard from Jerry Clayton.

"I do remember that when he told me, he was very distraught, very unhappy and, of course, I was too," said Strack, adding that he would have been pleased to trumpet the case for Etchberger receiving the Medal of Honor had he known about it.

"I wasn't fully aware of all of the circumstances of the time and the actions that were going on," he said. "I have on and off kind of known many of the chiefs of staff since then, but I just didn't know that this was something to be worked on and, of course, now I don't know any of those people. They are so far in my rear vision mirror that they probably weren't even in the Air Force when I retired."

Strack went to the Vietnam Veterans Memorial in Washington, D.C., after its 1982 dedication, touched Etchberger's name on the commemorative wall and said a prayer for him.

"There wasn't anything about him that was not laudatory," said the general. "He was not a very big man, but he was very, very imposing-looking in that he was groomed to perfection at all times. He was a picture of what you would want anyone to look like as a senior NCO or as an officer. Etch was capable of anything. In the final analysis, he could have been commander of the (Project Heavy Green) outfit. That's just the kind of a person that he had made himself. He was just that kind of a person. He obviously devoted himself to his country, to the Air Force, to his job, to his people."

Index

Matt Proietti

Matt Proietti